MUSSELS

BY THE *Kilted Chef,* **Alain Bossé,**

WITH A LITTLE HELP FROM HIS GOOD FRIEND,

Mussel Mama **Linda Duncan**

MUSSELS

PREPARING, COOKING *and* ENJOYING

a SENSATIONAL SEAFOOD

FOREWORD BY *Chef Michael Smith*

whitecap

Whitecap Books

First edition published 2014

Whitecap Books is known for its expertise in the cookbook market, and has produced some of
the most innovative and familiar titles found in kitchens across North America. Visit our website
at www.whitecap.ca.

EDITING: Theresa Best and Eva van Emden
DESIGN: Andrew Bagatella
FOOD PHOTOGRAPHY: Perry Jackson
FOOD STYLING: Alain Bossé
ADDITIONAL PHOTOGRAPHY: Mussel Industry Council (xi, top left and bottom right; 4, left; 30;
    41; 58; 67; 77; 87; 109; 132), Linda Duncan (3; 4, right) and Mylène Violette (169)
PROOFREADING: Steph Hill

Printed in Canada

Library and Archives Canada Cataloguing in Publication

Bossé, Alain, 1964-, author
    Mussels : preparing, cooking and enjoying a sensational
seafood / Alain Bossé and Linda Duncan.

Includes index.
ISBN 978-1-77050-214-7 (pbk.)

1. Cooking (Mussels). 2. Cookbooks. I. Duncan, Linda,
    1955-, author II. Title.

TX754.M98B68 2014   641.6'94   C2013-908280-8

The publisher acknowledges the financial support of the Government of Canada through the
Canada Book Fund (CBF) and the Province of British Columbia through the Book Publishing Tax
Credit.

14 15 16 17 18   5 4 3 2 1

This book was printed on chlorine-free paper
made with 10% post-consumer waste.

ALAIN

MY FATHER LEONARD passed before I became a chef but it was his example that taught me to work hard, be honest, and above all else, always have integrity. I lost him when I was seventeen but he's been in the kitchen with me for my whole career.

My beautiful mother Carmen unexpectedly passed in November of 2013. She was my biggest fan as I was hers. I miss her greatly but it's comforting to know that she now has a place in my kitchen alongside Dad.

To my partner Johanne; you are my support, my inspiration, and the compass that points me home. Need I say more? I love you forever plus one day.

LINDA

TO MY WONDERFUL husband Alan who not only eats everything I make but was up for tasting mussel recipes even for breakfast. For his endless hours of encouragement, being our non-cook proofreader and believing in me and this project.

To Fiona, my darling daughter, for testing recipes for us during this period and being our artist. Even in Ireland, she earnestly took part in this big family project.

CONTENTS

FOREWORD

MUSSELS ARE THE world's easiest seafood to cook and with this wonderful new cookbook they're even easier to add to your kitchen's repertoire! Whether you're a novice cook, amateur foodie, avid explorer or an experienced chef, this book is an indispensable resource for your kitchen. Jam packed with recipes, ideas, advice and stories it's sure to inspire and help you impress yourself in your own kitchen.

This book has three stars. No one knows mussels more than Chef Alain Bosse and 'Mussel Mama' Linda Duncan. They're the dream team and well known to all of us who are equally passionate about Atlantic Canada and our awesome ingredients. The authors share top billing with mussels from the pristine cold clear waters of Prince Edward Island though. The hard-working men and women of our fishing industry produce the best in the world!

As a passionate home cook, professional chef and avid cookbook writer I understand just how much passion and effort it takes to create a book like this. Alain and Linda have elevated the humble mussel by reminding us how simple and easy to cook they are, how they're inherently healthy and nutritious, how they're sustainably produced, how they're easy to find and affordable and perhaps most importantly how they're tasty and just plain delicious. Lets just say this book won't be sitting dusty on a shelf in my house, it's earned its rightful place on my counter where it's sure to get worn out from heavy use!

— Chef Michael Smith

PREFACE

THIS STORY STARTS with the humble mussel, a shellfish so unassuming that the impact it had on the two of us was quite unexpected. We (Alain Bossé, the "Kilted Chef", and Mussel Mama Linda Duncan) met each other on a cold winter night in Chicago. Passionate about mussels, and both involved in educating chefs and home cooks about their amazing attributes, we were lamenting that we couldn't get their great story out fast enough by meeting people face to face. We had been meeting and teaching culinary students and chefs, and showcasing mussels at consumer trade shows, at cooking classes and on local television shows for years, and we realized that the best way to get the word out about mussels was to do a cookbook.

This book is for those who are passionate about mussels and looking for new ways to cook and eat them, and for people who love mussels but only eat them in restaurants because they are not sure how to store and cook them at home. This book is also for the growing number of people who want a real connection with their food. We are no longer content to be strictly consumers but wish, in a sense, to be co-producers. Many of us want to know who grows our food, whether it is healthy and whether it is grown in a sustainable and ethical way. In this book, we not only share a variety of delicious recipes for every occasion, we tell you what you need to know to buy, store and cook mussels with confidence.

It has been such a pleasure to discover the story of the mussel and educating others has been part of our ongoing quest to learn more about the mussel ourselves. It has been a true delight to find fresh nuances and subtleties in cooking mussels—this pleasure is closest to a chef's heart.

It is our wish that you become as drawn to and inspired by mussels and the boundless possibilities they offer as we are.

Cheers,
Alain and Linda

INTRODUCTION

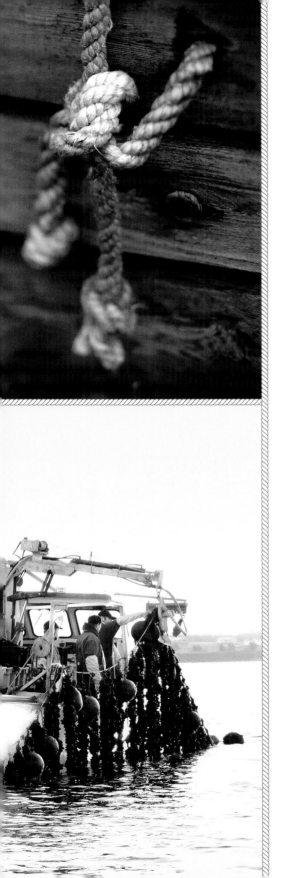

WHAT ARE MUSSELS?

A mussel is a bivalve, just like a clam, oyster or scallop, and grows in saltwater and freshwater in most parts of the world. The two halves of the mussel's shell are joined by a ligament and held shut by the adductor muscles inside the shell. Mussels have an extendable foot, which gives them limited mobility. To anchor themselves in place on rocks or other surfaces, they excrete a fluid which hardens in tough, silken threads commonly referred to as a mussel's "beard."

Most mussels that are available in our markets and restaurants today are saltwater mussels, which live in intertidal zones—areas that are underwater at high tide and exposed at low tide. Saltwater mussels can be found in every kind of habitat, from sheltered bays to exposed rocks. Freshwater mussels can be found in lakes, rivers and canals throughout the world. All mussels are filter-feeders—they filter water through their gills, separating the plankton from the water, and spit back out the particles they don't need.

One of the most common mussel species is the blue mussel, *Mytilus edulis*, which is native to the Atlantic coast and grows from the Virginia coastline to the Arctic as well as on the Pacific Coast of Canada and the US. Two closely related blue mussel species are *Mytilus trossulus*, found in the North Pacific and North Atlantic, and the Mediterranean mussel, *Mytilus galloprovincialis*. Other edible mussels

How Mussels Grow

Like all shellfish, mussels go through a life cycle. In the spring, they release millions of eggs and sperm into the water. As the sperm fertilize the eggs, mussel larvae are produced. The larvae float in the water for a short period of time, eventually looking for rough surfaces to attach to while they mature. The length of time it takes mussels to mature varies depending on the species, water temperature and food supply.

When mussels start their reproductive cycle, farmers set out rope for the larvae (the "seed") to attach to. Once on the rope, the seed is left to grow for approximately 6 months, after which the farmers take it to shore by boat. They then fill the socks with seed and tie the socks to the back line.

(Most farmers sort the seed by size, so that at harvest time the mussels can be sold by size. Too much variation in mussel size means that during cooking there is a risk that smaller mussels will be overcooked or larger ones undercooked.)

As the mussels start to grow, they move to the outside of the sock, hanging on by their beard threads, to be closer to the food supply (plankton and other microscopic organisms floating in the water). When they are about 2 inches (5 cm) long, usually when they are 18 to 24 months old, they are ready to be harvested.

include the California mussel, *Mytilus californianus*, native to the West Coast from Mexico to Alaska, and the greenshell mussel, *Perna canalicula*, from New Zealand. We have also seen the introduction of frozen Chilean blue mussels, *Mytilus chilensis*, in grocery stores in the last few years.

Blue mussels are farmed on the east and west coasts of North America and in China, Scandinavia, the Netherlands, the United Kingdom and the Mediterranean. The New Zealand greenshell mussel is farmed in both the North and South Island waters.

MUSSEL FARMING

Most of the mussels we eat are farmed. Different methods and techniques are used around the globe, depending on environmental conditions, regulations, salt levels and food sources within a region. In the Netherlands, for example, mussels are grown on the ocean bottom. The French use a system called *bouchot*, in which mussels are wrapped around oak posts and held in place with tubes. The Spanish have a raft system, with farms that may be some distance from the shore.

Here in North America, the most popular method is the long-line system, in which mussels spend their entire life cycle on lines suspended in the water. The long-line system has very little impact on the environment and is highly sustainable.

The Long-Line System

Mussels have been farmed for decades in different parts of the world; however, it wasn't until the 1970s that people in Atlantic Canada began to experiment with different techniques for growing mussels in the harsh conditions of that region. Ice coverage, cold temperatures and lack of detailed knowledge about feeding patterns were a few of the challenges the farmers faced. After experimention, they found the most effective system to be the long-line system, which had been initially developed by the Danish in the 1800s.

Mussels farmed using the long-line system are referred to as "rope grown"—they spend their whole lives attached to special ropes (called socks) that hang in the water and never touch the bottom. (Rope-grown mussels can also be labelled "cultured mussels" or "farmed mussels.")

The long-line system provides flexibility, allowing the grower to adapt to the seasons and tidal patterns, and to ensure the mussels have a good access to a food supply.

In the long-line system, a "backline" about 400 to 600 feet (120 to 180 m) long is suspended horizontally between two vertical lines. The vertical lines are attached to anchors on the ocean floor and marker buoys on the ocean surface. Another series of lines is attached at intervals to the back line and to more buoys on the ocean surface. This system keeps the back line horizontal and the socks suspended in position in the water column. The socks, made of plastic mesh, hang at intervals from the back line.

Cooks benefit from the long-line method of farming because it prevents grit or sand from getting into the mussels. They don't need to be soaked and there are no little pearls in the meat. Another advantage of this system is that it produces plumper mussels: there is more food in the water column than on the ocean floor, so mussels eat better. This system also keeps mussels away from predators such as

starfish and crabs, which lurk on the ocean bottom, and from seabirds, since the socks are not exposed to the air.

Farmed blue mussels are one of the great Canadian seafoods that we can be truly proud of. The majority of the fresh mussels that are eaten in North America come from Eastern Canada, with 75% to 80% coming from Prince Edward Island. It is no small feat that a little island only 140 miles (225 km) long can produce well over half of the mussels grown in Canada (Canada produced more than 62,000,000 pounds/28,100,000 kg of mussels in 2012). Mussels are also farmed in Nova Scotia, Newfoundland, Quebec, New Brunswick and British Columbia.

There are just over one hundred mussel farmers in PEI, who farm about 11,000 acres (4,500 hectares) of water in nineteen bays and estuaries. Their farms range from about 5 acres (2 hectares) of water being farmed part-time to 1,500-acre (600 hectare) operations with multiple boats and crews in several locations.

Farms are primarily family owned and multi-generational. The Fortunes, the Coles, the Rogerses, the Somerses, the Sullivans and the Stewarts are but a few of the family names often mentioned in the industry. Mussel farmers have a strong sense of stewardship, mentorship and investment, which has contributed to farms that produce high-quality, well-respected mussels. The industry is rural and provides employment year-round, which allows people to stay in their communities to make a living.

Farming mussels, like farming on land, means dealing with a large range of conditions and obstacles. Water temperatures in PEI vary from about 28°F (-2°C) in winter to up to 75°F (24°C) in the summer, meaning the mussels need to be hardy. Improvements in farming techniques are born out of a respectful working relationship between farmers and scientists as they continuously advance the industry.

Harvesting is done all year round, and

A Visit to a Mussel Farm

The first time Linda visited a mussel farm was when she went to Murray River, PEI, in 2007. She spent an afternoon with two pioneers of the industry, Ralph MacPherson and Carl Reynolds, visiting the seed lines and grow-out areas of their farms. It was a day that opened her eyes to the wonders and intricacies of mussel farming.

At that time, mussel farmers were having problems with sea squirts, which attach themselves to the lines, and looking for a way to get rid of them because they compete with mussels for the same food. Carl, a retired engineer, was full of ideas for equipment that could solve the problem. Ralph told Linda about changes in the farming process. When he first started his farm, there was very little to do after the lines were put out. Farmers simply came back 12 months later for the harvest. Today, mussel farmers, like farmers on land, tend their crop continuously, performing various husbandry tasks, such as spraying the mussel lines to remove fouling by competing species.

There was little sign of the farms nestled in the bays and rivers of the area except the marker buoys. All the long lines and mussel socks were out of sight below the water, and it was clear to Linda that respect for the environment was present and that the farms made little impact on the environment.

In her time working in the mussel industry, Linda has seen how hard-working, inventive and tenacious mussel farmers are. They have figured out how to use nature's bounty without harming the environment or disturbing any other species in the sea. They have sustainably refined their farming methods while at the same time preserving the health and well-being of the mussels.

Spending a working day on the water in PEI is an amazing privilege. Each time Linda has the chance to spend time on the mussel farms, she has come away with profound respect for these farmers of the sea.

mussel aquaculture is not governed by the rules of traditional fisheries. In PEI, for example, there are no quotas, so farmers can grow and harvest their crops as orders are received and there is no waste. The result is a supply of freshly harvested mussels available 12 months of the year.

From April to December, harvesting is done by boat. The socks are cut from the back lines, stored in insulated tanks and delivered to the wharf. In the winter months, from January through March, harvesting is much more complicated and dangerous as the mussel farms are covered in ice. When the ice is 12 to 14 inches (30 to 35 cm) thick, farmers use trucks or tractors to plow an ice road to drive out to their leases, which can be up to 2 miles (3 km) from shore. Farmers must wear survival suits in case they break through the ice and also to protect them from the bitter cold. After using either divers or GPS systems to locate the long lines, the farmer cuts a hole in the ice using a special chainsaw. The long line is hauled up and each mussel sock is cut off and immediately placed in an insulated tank to prevent it from freezing.

At the mussel processing plant, the mussel clumps are separated and mussel sock removed. The mussels are then washed and polished to remove any barnacles that have formed on the mussel shells and the beards are removed. The mussels are individually inspected for broken or damaged shells and packaged in preparation for being sold at markets.

HOW TO CHOOSE QUALITY MUSSELS
Farmed versus Wild Mussels
In Canada, most of the fresh mussels that you will find are PEI mussels, which are readily available at the fish counter of most supermarkets or at seafood markets. Farmed mussels are usually free of grit and uniformly sized.

Wild mussels, which most often come from Maine, are harvested by gently dragging the bottom of the ocean. Ususally they have not been sorted by size. They contain sand and grit, which must be removed before cooking (soaking them in water with salt, corn flour or flour might help remove the grit).

If you buy mussels from a reputable place, you can be confident that they are safe to eat. If you gather wild mussels yourself, be sure to look for notices on the beachfront warning of water contamination.

Buying Fresh Mussels
To get the best mussels, buy them from a reputable store and develop a good rapport with the counter staff. Mussels are usually sold loose or in mesh bags, weighing 2 or 5 pounds (1 or 2.2 kg). Look carefully at how they are displayed. Are they wet and shiny, and is their shell colour a blackish blue? These are the key signs of mussels that have been well cared for. Mussels should be kept on a bed of ice and may even have ice on top. Ask to smell a couple. If they smell like the ocean, they are fresh. If they smell fishy, don't buy them! Ask the counter staff to give you mussels that have the most recent harvest date indicated.

Fresh mussels are regulated by the Canadian Food Inspection Agency (CFIA) or the US Food and Drug Administration (FDA) with a tagging system that tracks mussels through the supply chain. The tag records when the mussels were harvested, where the mussels were grown and when they were shipped. If you don't see the tag, ask the counter staff to show you the tag;

they are required to keep them.

Generally, mussels are great to eat up to 7 to 14 days from being harvested. Check the tag to see how long ago the mussels were harvested and, therefore, how long you can store them at home. Depending on the date and how well they have been cared for, you don't have to use mussels right away. You can buy them ahead of time and store them in the refrigerator for a few days before cooking.

High-Oxygen Storage

You might find fresh mussels in high-oxygen trays or bags. In this packaging method oxygen is injected into the package to put the mussels into a dormant state, extending their shelf life. Do not freeze this package when you get home. You may find that a number of the mussels are slightly open; rinse them vigorously under fresh water to wake them up, and set them aside for 10 minutes before you cook them to help them close up again. Discard any that do not close. The cooking methods for mussels sold in this packaging are exactly the same as for fresh mussels.

Frozen Mussels

The selection of mussels is usually widest in the frozen mussel section of the market, with the most prominent variety being New Zealand greenshell mussels. Check the best-before date and follow the preparation instructions on the packaging.

When to Buy

These days, fresh mussels are available all year round. For a few months after mussels release their eggs and sperm, they lose some of their body mass and the mussel meat will be smaller in the shell. This phenomenon occurs at different times of year, depending on where the mussels are grown and the water temperature. This has no effect on the flavour or texture of the mussels.

We want to debunk the myth that you should only buy mussels when there's an R in the month. The origin of this belief is unknown but probably comes from a number of factors: with poor refrigeration mussels spoil more quickly in warm weather, wild mussels usually spawn in the summer months and red tides are more common in the summer.

The term "red tide" describes a bloom of harmful algae. These blooms occur nearly every summer along both coasts of North America, when algae grow out of control, and can have a toxic effect on people, fish, shellfish, marine mammals and birds. Shellfish from a red tide can be poisonous and, although rare, the sickness that results from eating it can can be debilitating and even fatal. If your mussels come from a commercially inspected plant, which will have water testing done, you can be sure that they are safe.

STORING MUSSELS AT HOME

Once you get your fresh mussels home, remove them from the mesh bag, if they are in one, and place them in a bowl covered with a damp cloth to keep them moist. Some people like to put the mussels inside a colander in the bowl for easier drainage. Put them at the back of the refrigerator, where it tends to be the coolest, as they are happiest at 39°F to 43°F (4°C to 6°C). Don't worry if you see water accumulate in the bowl. That's perfectly normal. Just remember to drain the water every day. Never submerge live mussels in fresh water for very long, or these delicate sea creatures will die.

HOW TO PREPARE AND COOK MUSSELS

Because mussels are cooked live, be careful how you prepare and cook them.

First, determine which of the mussels you've bought are suitable for cooking. Place the mussels in a colander and rinse them under cold running tap water. Sometimes there are some mussels that are slightly open (we call these "gapers"), which need to be woken up. If the shell is open, simply tap the mussel firmly against the side of the counter: if the mussel is still living, it will close. If it doesn't close, discard it. Discard any mussels with broken shells.

The best indicator that mussels are cooked is that their shells are open. If the mussels are undercooked, the meat will stick to the shell and be both unappealing and difficult to eat. If they are overcooked, the meat will shrink and be tough. After cooking, you might have a few that didn't open; throw these away.

In short: if your mussels don't close before you cook them, throw them away. If your mussels don't open when you cook them, throw them away.

Suggested Cooking Times for Mussels

Amount of mussels	Amount of liquid suggested	Approximate cooking time
1 pound (500 g)	¼ cup (60 mL)	4 to 5 minutes
2 pounds (1 kg)	½ cup (125 mL)	5 to 6 minutes
5 pounds (2.2 kg)	½ cup (125 mL)	6 to 8 minutes
10 pounds (4.5 kg)	1 cup (250 mL)	8 to 10 minutes

Choosing a Cooking Liquid

The list of liquids you can use to steam mussels is endless. The most common is white wine. Red wine is seldom used as its strong flavour competes with the gentle flavour of the mussels. If you like beer, we suggest you use a lighter beer unless you are a big fan of heavier beer, in which case we say, "fill your boots" (a common Maritime expression). Some people like to add spirits such as Pernod, tequila, vermouth, vodka and sambuca.

For those of you who prefer a non-alcoholic cooking liquid, we suggest water, apple juice, apple cider and citrus juices. Even some soft drinks like root beer work really well.

Cooking the Mussels

To cook mussels, you need only three things: mussels, a small amount of liquid and a pot with a lid. Mussels are cooked by steaming, not boiling. All you do is add the liquid and mussels to the pot, cover it, and turn the heat up to high. When steam pours out from under the lid, the mussels are done. Don't peek to see how they are doing while they are cooking, because the more you lift the lid, the more steam escapes, which means that mussels will take longer to cook and the meats will shrink.

If you have mussels and broth left over, you can freeze them in a covered dish or sealed plastic bag. Make sure to cover the mussels with the broth, and they will keep in the freezer for two to three months.

Cooking times will vary slightly, depending on the kind of heat you are using; the times above are based on the highest heat on your stovetop. The fail-safe test is that when steam is pouring out from under the lid, the mussels are ready to eat. The amount of liquid suggested should cover the bottom of the pot.

HOW TO EAT MUSSELS

So you thought there was only one way to eat your mussels . . . Well, here are a few fun ways to eat or treat your mussels:

Traditional: Just use your fingers to pull the mussel meat out of the shell. There is something wonderful about licking the juice off your fingers. For those who don't like getting their fingers dirty, a fork works well to dig out the mussel meat.

Mussel shucker: Some people like to take the meat out of all the mussel shells, pop it into the broth and sip it all together like a soup.

Mussel tongs: Take a mussel shell, pull out the mussel meat, eat it, and then use the shell as pinchers to eat the rest of the mussels in the bowl.

Mussel ring: As you eat each mussel, place the shell inside your last mussel shell to form a ring. Linda's family likes to make mussel lines—pick a pattern and see who can make the largest circle.

Mussel spork: Break your mussel shell into two pieces. Grab your fork and hold it upright. Take the bottom shell, which has a deeper cup, and hook it onto the tongs on the end of your fork. Now use your mussel spoon to slurp up all the broth.

HOW MANY MUSSELS TO SERVE

Knowing how many mussels you need to serve your guests will ensure a successful event. The general rule of thumb is 1 to 1¼ lb (500 to 625 g) per person for a main course, and ½ lb (250 g) per person for an appetizer. You can expect about ¾ to 1 cup (160 to 250 mL) of broth for each pound of mussels you cook. For dishes that require you to use the shells, expect to find about 20 to 22 mussels in a pound (500 g).

If you have a recipe that calls for mussel meat, we suggest that each pound (500 g) of mussels will produce approximately 3 to 4 oz (85 to 125 g) of mussel meat.

This amount varies slightly depending on the time of the year. When the meat from individual mussels is smaller in the summer months, you may need 1½ lb (750 g) of mussels for the same yield of meat.

NUTRITIONAL PROPERTIES OF MUSSELS

Mussels are a nutritional powerhouse. They are loaded with vitamins and nutrients. The specific nutritional breakdown varies between mussel species and even from one season to the other. PEI blue mussels contain fewer than 150 calories in a 1 lb (500 g) serving (about 3 to 4 oz/85 to 115 g shelled) with less

than 5 grams of fat and 24 to 28 grams of protein, which makes these mussels a very low-fat protein choice. In general, mussels are high in iron, phosphorus, manganese, vitamin B12, and even vitamin C, which is rare among protein sources. Mussels are also an excellent source of selenium, a dietary antioxidant involved in the formation of a protein that defends against oxidative stress.

Lastly, for those of you who are looking for gluten-free recipes, you will be pleased to know that mussels fit this category.

ABOUT THE INGREDIENTS

There are many ingredients used in the recipes in this cookbook. Please use the following as our general guide. We want these recipes to be an inspiration to you, the home cook, so substituting items you have in your cupboard for the ingredients listed in the recipe is perfectly acceptable. For example, if a recipe calls for shallots and you don't have them, use whichever onion you have on hand.

- OIL We prefer canola oil as basic vegetable oil, but others will work just fine. When a recipe calls for olive oil, use extra virgin olive oil.

- PEPPER Freshly ground pepper is our choice.

- HERBS Our preference is for fresh herbs, although we realize that they are not always available. If you substitute dry herbs, use a little less.

- MOLASSES Both cooking and fancy molasses will work for the recipes in this book.

- CITRUS JUICE Please use fresh citrus juice whenever possible. Processed juice sometimes has artificial flavours.

- BREADCRUMBS We use dry, unseasoned crumbs unless indicated differently.

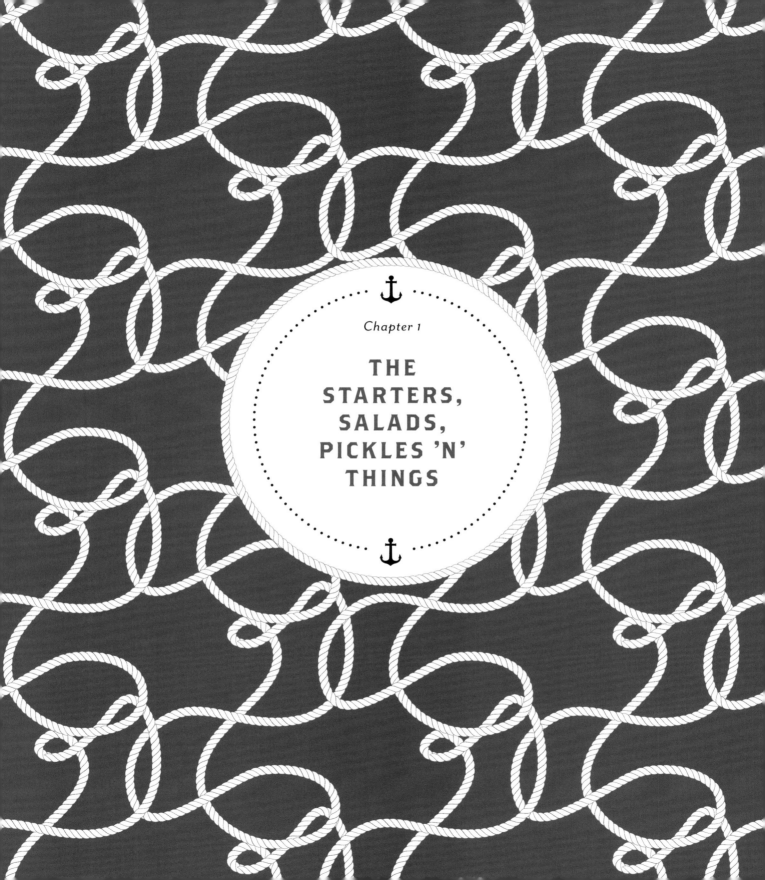

Chapter 1

THE STARTERS, SALADS, PICKLES 'N' THINGS

TACOS

with Tequila-Flavoured Mussels and Black Bean Salsa

{Serves 6}

MUSSELS

2½ lb (1.25 kg) mussels

2 oz (60 mL) tequila

juice of half a lime

2 green onions, chopped

SALSA

one 14 oz (398 mL) can of black
  beans, rinsed

1 cup (250 mL) corn kernels

2 cups (500 mL) fresh diced
  tomatoes

¼ cup (60 mL) red diced onion

½ cup (125 mL) chopped cilantro

3 Tbsp (45 mL) olive oil

1 tsp (5 mL) coarse salt

½ tsp (2.5 mL) ground black
  pepper

juice of 1 lemon

juice of 1 lime

ASSEMBLY

12 taco shells

1 head iceberg lettuce, shredded

1 cup (250 mL) grated old
  cheddar cheese

1 cup (250 mL) sour cream

6 green onions, chopped

TACOS ARE SUCH a great solution to those hectic weeknights when you're trying to juggle dinner with late nights in the office, last-minute deadlines and laundry. The mussels and salsa can be prepared in advance so all that's left is the assembly. Add a salad, and you have a meal that's quick, nutritious and delicious.

MUSSELS

1 Rinse the mussels under running fresh water. Throw away any that do not close.

2 In a large pot, add the mussels, tequila, lime juice and green onions. Cover with a lid and cook on high for approximately 5 to 6 minutes or until steam is pouring out from under the lid.

3 Let the mussels cool. Remove the mussel meat from the shells and discard the shells. Refrigerate until ready to assemble.

SALSA

4 In a large bowl, add the beans, corn, tomatoes, onions, cilantro, olive oil, salt, pepper, lemon and lime and stir well to combine. Refrigerate for at least 30 minutes.

ASSEMBLY

5 Line up 6 bowls on the counter and fill each with one of the filling components: cooked mussels, salsa, shredded iceberg lettuce, grated cheddar cheese, sour cream and chopped green onions. Take a taco shell and fill it with a small amount of each filling. Repeat with the remaining 11 taco shells. Serve immediately.

MUSSEL AND CORN FRITTERS

with Creamy Dill Remoulade

{Serves 6 as a main course or 24 as an hors d'oeuvre}

DILL REMOULADE

2 tsp (10 mL) finely chopped
   fresh dill

2 tsp (10 mL) lemon juice

2 tsp (10 mL) lime juice

2 Tbsp (30 mL) finely diced
   shallots

¾ cup (185 mL) mayonnaise

salt and pepper to taste

MUSSEL FRITTERS

2 lb (1 kg) mussels

¼ cup (60 mL) white wine

1½ cups (375 mL) flour

1 tsp (5 mL) salt

2 tsp (10 mL) baking powder

1 egg, lightly beaten

1 cup (250 mL) whole milk

¼ cup (60 mL) finely diced red
   pepper

¼ cup (60 mL) finely diced
   shallots

1 cup (250 mL) corn kernels

4 cups (1 L) vegetable oil

ALMOST EVERY COUNTRY has a version of a fritter. They are always deep-fried and contain meat, seafood, fruit or vegetables. This one is a take on a southern corn fritter, and we think the mussels along with the dill remoulade make them exceptionally flavourful.

DILL REMOULADE

1   In a bowl, mix the dill, lemon juice, lime juice, shallots, mayonnaise, and salt and pepper together. Cover with plastic wrap and refrigerate until ready to use.

MUSSEL FRITTERS

2   Rinse the mussels under running fresh water. Throw away any that do not close.

3   In a large pot, add the mussels and wine. Cover with a lid and cook on high for approximately 5 to 6 minutes or until steam is pouring out from under the lid.

4   Let the mussels cool. Remove the mussel meat from the shells and put it in a covered bowl or dish.

5   Mix the flour, salt, and baking powder together in a large bowl. Make a well in the centre and add the egg and milk. Whisk, making sure that no lumps remain. Mix in the red pepper, shallots, corn and mussel meat.

6   Add the vegetable oil to a deep fryer and heat to 350°F (175°C). Using a tablespoon, carefully drop the fritters one by one into the hot oil. Cook until golden brown, about 5 minutes. Remove with a slotted spoon and place on a paper towel.

7   Serve the fritters with the dill remoulade on the side for dipping.

MUSSEL SALAD AL FRESCO

{Serves 4}

MUSSELS

2½ lb (1.25 kg) mussels

½ cup (125 mL) white wine

2 green onions, chopped

2 cloves garlic, finely chopped

1 lemon, cut in half

VINAIGRETTE

¼ cup (60 mL) white wine
  vinegar

½ cup (125 mL) olive oil

4 sprigs parsley, chopped

2 cloves garlic, minced

salt and ground black pepper
  to taste

ASSEMBLY

1 romaine lettuce heart, sliced
  lengthwise in quarters

2 cups (500 mL) halved cherry
  tomatoes

¼ cup (60 mL) bite-sized pieces
  cooked double-smoked bacon

½ medium red onion, julienne

¼ cup (60 mL) shaved fresh
  Parmesan cheese

ALAIN LOVES THE freshness that the parsley vinaigrette brings to this salad. Combine the salad with larger chunks of vegetables and you have a winning combination for a barbecue.

MUSSELS

1 Rinse the mussels under running fresh water. Throw away any that do not close.

2 In a large pot, add the mussels, wine, green onions and garlic. Squeeze one lemon half over the mussels and drop the rind into the pot. Cover with a lid, and cook on high for approximately 5 to 6 minutes or until steam is pouring out from under the lid.

3 Let the mussels cool. Remove the mussel meat from the shells and put it in a covered bowl or dish.

4 Refrigerate until ready to assemble.

VINAIGRETTE

5 In a small jar with a tightly fitting lid, combine the wine vinegar, olive oil, parsley, garlic, salt, pepper and the juice of the other half of the lemon. Shake well. Refrigerate for one hour before serving. (This dressing will keep for 10 to 14 days in the refrigerator.)

ASSEMBLY

6 Place the romaine on a large platter.

7 In a bowl, combine the cooked mussel meat, tomatoes, bacon and onion. Arrange the mussel mixture overtop of the lettuce. Pour the vinaigrette overtop. Garnish with the Parmesan cheese shavings.

SUMMER FIG AND MUSSEL SALAD

{Serves 4}

MUSSELS
2 lb (1 kg) mussels

¼ cup (60 mL) white wine

DRESSING
1 Tbsp (15 mL) lemon juice

1 Tbsp (15 mL) red wine vinegar

3 Tbsp (45 mL) canola oil

1 tsp (5 mL) Dijon mustard

salt and pepper to taste

THIS RECIPE IS great for summer when fresh figs are at their best, and with a little bread and a glass of wine, it makes a complete meal. The wonderful flavours of figs and mussels balance well with the saltiness of the Parmesan cheese and prosciutto. Make sure that you ask for very thinly sliced prosciutto at your deli counter.

MUSSELS

1   Rinse the mussels under running fresh water. Throw away any that do not close.

2   In a large pot, add ¼ cup (60 mL) of wine and the mussels. Cover with a lid and cook on high for approximately 5 to 6 minutes or until steam is pouring out from under the lid.

3   Let the mussels cool. Remove the mussel meat from the shells and put it in a covered bowl or dish.

4   Refrigerate until ready to assemble.

DRESSING

5   While the mussels are cooking, place the lemon juice, wine vinegar, oil, mustard, and salt and pepper in a small glass or plastic container and shake vigorously. Set aside.

6   Pour the dressing over the mussels, cover and put in the refrigerator. This can be done several hours before you want to serve the dish.

SALAD

4 figs

2 cups (500 mL) arugula

2 slices prosciutto

¼ cup (60 mL) shaved Parmesan
  cheese

¼ cup (60 mL) toasted and
  roughly chopped almonds

SALAD

7   Cut the figs in quarters. Cut the prosciutto into thin
strips.

8   On four plates, arrange the arugula, prosciutto, mussels
and figs with the flesh side outward. Drizzle the dressing
over the salad. Finish it off with the slivers of Parmesan
cheese and the almonds.

⚓
MUSSEL CEVICHE
{Serves 4}

2 lb (1 kg) fresh mussels

¼ cup (60 mL) white wine

1 cup (250 mL) fresh corn kernels

½ cup (125 mL) diced red onion

½ cup (125 mL) diced yellow
   pepper

1 tsp (5 mL) coarse salt

1 tsp (5 mL) ground pepper

1 hot chili pepper, seeds removed
   and finely diced

4 Tbsp (60 mL) chopped cilantro

juice of 1 lime

4 leaves of bibb lettuce

CEVICHE, A DISH of raw fish marinated in citrus, is found throughout Latin America and is very commonly associated with Peru. In North America, ceviche is frequently made with scallops. The traditional lime flavour of ceviche pairs beautifully with raw fish, but we've chosen to do our own take on the dish by using steamed mussels. For a unique presentation, serve the ceviche in individual martini glasses.

1   Rinse the mussels under running fresh water. Throw away any that do not close.

2   In a large pot, add the mussels and wine. Cover with a lid and cook on high heat for approximately 5 to 6 minutes or until steam is pouring out from under the lid.

3   Let the mussels cool. Remove the mussel meat from the shells and discard the shells.

4   Refrigerate until ready to assemble.

5   In a large bowl, add the mussel meat with the corn, red onion and yellow pepper; toss gently to avoid breaking the mussel meat. Add the salt, pepper, chili pepper and cilantro and toss. Refrigerate.

6   Just before serving, add half a cup (125 mL) of the reserved mussel broth and lime juice and mix.

7   Place a leaf of lettuce on a plate. Take a scoop of ceviche and gently mound it over top.

MUSSEL AND LOBSTER BRUSCHETTA

{Serves 4}

2 lb (1 kg) fresh mussels

¼ cup (60 mL) white wine

¼ medium red onion, finely
chopped

12 fresh basil leaves, coarsely
chopped, plus 4 leaves for
garnish

1 tsp (5 mL) coarse salt

1 tsp (5 mL) ground pepper

2 cloves garlic, grated

½ cup (125 mL) olive oil

juice of 1 lemon

½ lb (250 g) pre-cooked lobster
meat (or thawed frozen
lobster meat)

4 slices of crusty bread

2 Tbsp (30 mL) Maître d'Hôtel
Butter (page 179) or regular
butter

THIS TAKE ON traditional bruschetta, substituting lobster and mussels for tomatoes, is always met with surprise. Alain has never come across mussel bruschetta anywhere else, nor have many of his guests, but it is always a big hit, and it's one of his most requested recipes. The Maître d'Hôtel Butter (page 179) is a herbed butter that adds another level of flavour. Regular butter can be substituted, but the extra time needed to make this version is worth the effort.

∎   ∎

1   Rinse the mussels under running fresh water. Throw away any that do not close.

2   In a large pot, add the mussels and wine. Cover with a lid and cook on high for approximately 5 to 6 minutes or until steam is pouring out from under the lid.

3   Let the mussels cool. Remove the mussel meat from the shells and put it in a covered bowl or dish.

4   Refrigerate until ready to assemble.

5   Place the red onion, chopped basil, salt, pepper, garlic, olive oil and lemon juice in a large bowl and mix well. Chop the lobster meat into 1-inch (2.5 cm) chunks. Add the cooked mussel meat and the lobster meat and toss gently. Refrigerate for at least 30 minutes.

6   Butter both sides of each slice of the bread and grill in a dry frying pan until golden brown and crisp on both sides.

7   To assemble, place the grilled bread on a plate and top with the bruschetta mixture. Serve garnished with a basil leaf.

CALIFORNIA-STYLE MUSSEL

and Avocado Salsa on Grilled Polenta

{Serves 4}

5 lb (2.2 kg) fresh mussels

½ cup (125 mL) white wine

2 tomatoes, seeded and diced

1 avocado, chopped

1 garlic clove, minced

¼ cup (60 mL) diced red onions

¼ cup (60 mL) chopped cilantro

juice of 2 limes

½ tsp (2.5 mL) Sriracha sauce

salt and pepper to taste

8 grilled polenta cakes
  (see Savoury Polenta Cakes,
  page 167)

½ cup (125 mL) crumbled
  goat cheese

4 sprigs cilantro, for garnish

THIS IS ONE of Alain's favourite recipes. Both parts of the recipe are very versatile. He has served it as an appetizer, but also finds that it is perfect as a light lunch. Make sure your avocado is not too ripe; you will want it to be nice and firm. The salsa can be made ahead, as the lime juice will help it retain its vibrant green colour.

1   Rinse the mussels under running fresh water. Throw away any that do not close.

2   In a large pot, add the mussels and wine. Cover with a lid and cook on high for approximately 6 to 8 minutes or until steam is pouring out from under the lid.

3   Let the mussels cool. Remove the mussel meat from the shells and put it in a covered bowl or dish.

4   Refrigerate until ready to assemble.

5   In a large bowl, toss the tomatoes, avocado, garlic, onions, cilantro, lime juice, Sriracha sauce, and salt and pepper. Gently stir in the mussels and refrigerate until ready to serve.

6   Prepare the grilled Polenta Cakes (page 167). Place two triangles in the centre of each plate. Then mound the prepared salsa on top, add the crumbled goat cheese and garnish with a sprig of cilantro.

GREEK-STYLE MUSSEL
and Watermelon Salad
{Serves 6}

MUSSELS

2 lb (1 kg) mussels

¼ cup (60 mL) white wine

SALAD

4 cups (1 L) 1½-inch (4 cm)
  watermelon cubes

½ red onion, julienne

1 English cucumber, diced

24 oregano leaves

24 basil leaves, chopped

24 pitted kalamata olives

½ cup (125 mL) olive oil

¼ cup (60 mL) white balsamic
  vinegar

1½ Tbsp (22.5 mL) coarse salt

1 Tbsp (15 mL) black pepper

½ cup (125 mL) crumbled
  feta cheese

IS THERE ANYTHING more refreshing than a cool slice of watermelon on a hot summer's day? Alain thinks this mussel and watermelon salad makes a pretty refreshing change from a traditional garden salad. The sweetness of the watermelon balances the saltiness of the mussels and feta, creating a perfect balance on the palate.

MUSSELS

1 Rinse the mussels under running fresh water. Throw away any that do not close.

2 In a large pot, add the mussels and wine. Cover with a lid and cook on high for approximately 5 to 6 minutes or until steam is pouring out from under the lid.

3 Let the mussels cool. Remove the mussel meat from the shells and put it in a covered bowl or dish.

4 Refrigerate until ready to assemble.

SALAD

5 In a large bowl, toss the watermelon, red onion, cucumber, oregano, basil, and olives. Pour in the olive oil, vinegar, salt and pepper and mix until incorporated. Carefully fold in the mussels and top with the feta cheese.

6 Refrigerate for at least one hour. Gently re-toss just before serving.

CITRUS HONEY MUSSEL SALAD

{Serves 4 as an appetizer or 2 as a meal}

SALAD

2 lb (1 kg) mussels

¼ cup (60 mL) white wine

½ cup (125 mL) arugula

¼ cup (60 mL) diced yellow
  peppers

¼ cup (60 mL) diced red peppers

¼ cup (60 mL) diced red onions

VINAIGRETTE

½ shallot, finely diced

½ cup (125 mL) honey

½ cup (125 mL) lemon juice

zest of half a lime

juice of 1 lime

½ cup (125 mL) canola oil

1 Tbsp (15 mL) Dijon mustard

1 Tbsp (15 mL) finely chopped
  Italian parsley (or chives)

CITRUS IS A natural pairing with mussels—when we think of additions to mussels, what comes to mind is freshly squeezed lemon—but the sweetness of honey also marries beautifully. Adding mussels to salad is a wonderful way to take it from appetizer to meal. Add a crisp white wine and crusty bread, and this salad is the perfect dish to serve for a late morning brunch or afternoon luncheon.

SALAD

1   Rinse the mussels under running fresh water. Throw away any that do not close.

2   In a large pot, add the mussels and wine. Cover with a lid and cook on high for approximately 5 to 6 minutes or until steam is coming out from under the lid.

3   Let the mussels cool. Remove the mussel meat from the shells and put it in a covered bowl or dish.

4   Refrigerate until ready to assemble.

VINAIGRETTE

5   Combine the shallot, honey, lemon juice, lime zest, lime juice, oil, mustard and parsley (or chives) in a Mason jar or other glass jar with a tightly fitting lid and shake vigorously, or if you prefer, whisk together in a bowl until they emulsify.

6   Refrigerate for one hour before serving. The vinaigrette will keep for 10 to 14 days in the refrigerator.

ASSEMBLY

7   Divide the arugula between the plates and top with the diced peppers and onions. Divide the chilled mussel meat between the plates, and drizzle with the citrus honey vinaigrette.

WARM MUSSEL POTATO SALAD

{Serves 8}

MUSSELS

3 lb (1.5 kg) mussels

¼ cup (60 mL) white wine

SALAD

3 cups (750 mL) 1-inch (2.5 cm)
  cubed red potato

1 garlic clove, finely diced

⅛ cup (30 mL) finely diced
  shallots

pinch of salt

1 red onion, thinly sliced

ALTHOUGH LINDA WAS raised with only a cold, creamy mayonnaise-based sauce on potato salad, she prefers this warm German-style dressing that is influenced by her years of living in Europe. The recipe is for a warm salad, but it tastes just as good cold. This salad looks great served on a bed of arugula in a bowl or on a platter.

MUSSELS

1 Rinse the mussels under running fresh water. Throw away any that do not close.

2 In a large pot, add the mussels and wine. Cover with a lid and cook on high for approximately 5 to 6 minutes or until steam is pouring out from under the lid.

3 Let the mussels cool. Remove the mussel meat from the shells and put it in a covered bowl or dish. Reserve 2 Tbsp (60 mL) of the broth.

4 Refrigerate until ready to assemble.

SALAD

5 Cook the potatoes and salt in a saucepan until just tender. Take off the heat and drain.

6 Put the red onion in ice-cold water to soak. This will tame the bite of the raw onions and soften their flavour.

DRESSING

¼ cup (60 mL) olive oil

2 Tbsp (30 mL) sherry vinegar

2 Tbsp (30 mL) mussel broth

2 tsp (10 mL) grainy Dijon
    mustard

2 Tbsp (30 mL) white sugar

1 tsp (5 mL) horseradish

2 heaping Tbsp (35 mL) capers

DRESSING

7 In a small bowl, whisk the olive oil, vinegar, mussel broth,
   mustard, sugar, horseradish and capers together until thick.

ASSEMBLY

8 In a large bowl, add the potatoes, garlic, shallots and red
   onion.

9 Add the mussels. Pour on the dressing and toss very gently.

TABBOULEH MUSSEL SALAD

with Orzo

{Serves 6}

MUSSELS

2 lb (1 kg) mussels

¼ cup (60 mL) white wine

ORZO

3 cups water

1 tsp (5 mL) salt

1 cup (250 mL) raw orzo

SALAD

2 cups (500 mL) finely chopped
fresh parsley

1½ cups (375 mL) finely diced
fresh tomatoes

½ cup (125 mL) finely diced red
onions

18 mint leaves, chopped

juice of 4 lemons

⅓ cup (80 mL) olive oil

1 tsp (5 mL) salt

½ tsp (2.5 mL) ground pepper

TABBOULEH IS A salad that originates in the Middle East and is quite often part of *meze*, a series of small dishes served for breakfast or lunch. Typically, tabbouleh is made with bulgur wheat or couscous. The introduction of orzo and mussels makes it unique and very tasty!

MUSSELS

1 Rinse the mussels under running fresh water. Throw away any that do not close.

2 In a large pot, add the mussels and wine. Cover with a lid and cook on high for approximately 5 to 6 minutes or until steam is pouring out from under the lid.

3 Let the mussels cool. Remove the mussel meat from the shells and put it in a covered bowl or dish.

4 Refrigerate until ready to assemble.

ORZO

5 In a medium pot, add the water and salt and bring to a boil.

6 Add the orzo, cover and cook uncovered for 7 to 8 minutes. Stir occasionally. Set aside to cool.

SALAD

7 Toss the parsley, tomatoes, red onions and mint together in a medium bowl, then add the lemon juice, olive oil, and salt and pepper. Once everything is well mixed, lightly toss in the mussels and the orzo.

8 Refrigerate for at least one hour, and gently re-toss before serving.

SMOKED MUSSEL SALAD
with Goat Cheese Crostini
{Serves 4}

MUSSELS

2½ lb (1.25 kg) mussels

¾ cup (185 mL) beer

1 garlic clove, minced

handful of wood chips

SALAD

¼ cup (60 mL) julienne red
    pepper

¼ cup (60 mL) julienne yellow
    pepper

24 cherry tomatoes, cut in half

12 sweet basil leaves, torn

salt and pepper to taste

Taking a little extra time to smoke the mussel meat adds a wonderful flavour and sets this dish apart. It also shows how simple the process of smoking foods at home is. It's a skill that we are sure you'll use time and again. Alain prefers to use maple wood chips, but if you like an extra smoky flavour, try cedar or hickory chips.

■ ▬▬▬▬▬▬▬▬▬▬ ■

MUSSELS

1. Rinse the mussels under running fresh water. Throw away any that do not close.

2. In a large pot, add the mussels, beer and garlic. Cover with a lid and cook on high for approximately 5 to 7 minutes or until steam is pouring out from under the lid.

3. Let the mussels cool. Remove the mussel meat from the shells and put it in a covered bowl or dish.

4. Refrigerate until ready to assemble.

5. Line a deep roasting pan with a 12 × 12-inch (30 × 30 cm) piece of foil, and place the wood chips on top.

6. Wrap a cooling rack in foil. Make a few small holes in the foil and place the rack on top of the wood chips. Place the mussel meat on the rack. Have a piece of foil ready to cover the pan, and then use a match to light the wood chips. Cover tightly.

7. Allow to smoke for 10 to 15 minutes and then remove the cover. If you find that the smoky flavour is too mild, simply add a bit more wood and repeat. This process can be done outdoors if you wish.

8. Refrigerate until ready to serve.

DRESSING

¾ cup (185 mL) olive oil

4 Tbsp (60 mL) balsamic vinegar

4 Tbsp (60 mL) maple syrup

ASSEMBLY

1 cup (250 mL) mixed greens

SALAD

9 In a large bowl, mix the red and yellow peppers, tomatoes and basil. Season with salt and pepper to taste.

DRESSING

10 Place the olive oil, balsamic vinegar and maple syrup in a jar with a tightly fitting lid and shake vigorously.

ASSEMBLY

11 Divide the mixed greens between four plates, top with the mussel salad and drizzle with the vinaigrette.

12 Serve with Goat Cheese Crostini (page 176)

QUINOA MUSSEL SALAD

{Serves 6}

MUSSELS

2 lb (1 kg) mussels

¼ cup (60 mL) white wine

QUINOA

1 cup (250 mL) quinoa

1 ¾ cups reserved mussel broth

DRESSING

1 garlic clove, minced

1 Tbsp (15 mL) Dijon mustard

¾ cup (185 mL) olive oil

¼ cup (60 mL) white balsamic
   vinegar

¼ cup (60 mL) maple syrup

QUINOA HAS MADE a huge surge in popularity, and no wonder: it's both healthy and delicious. Even if the brand you buy is labelled "pre-rinsed," we highly recommend rinsing the quinoa to make sure it is not bitter.

■━━━━━━■

MUSSELS

1 Rinse the mussels under running fresh water. Throw away any that do not close.

2 In a large pot, add the mussels and wine. Cover with a lid and cook on high for approximately 5 to 6 minutes or until steam is pouring out from under the lid.

3 Let the mussels cool. Remove the mussel meat from the shells and put it in a covered bowl or dish. Reserve 1¾ cups (435 mL) of the broth.

4 Refrigerate until ready to assemble.

QUINOA

5 Thoroughly rinse the quinoa and set aside.

6 Bring the mussel broth to a simmer over medium heat. Stir in the quinoa, cover and allow to simmer until the liquid is absorbed, approximately 12 minutes.

7 When the liquid is all gone, use a fork to fluff the quinoa, put the lid back on and set aside for 5 minutes.

8 Spread the quinoa out on a baking sheet and allow it to cool completely. Refrigerate until needed.

SALAD

1 cup (250 mL) halved cherry
  tomatoes
1 English cucumber, finely diced
1 orange pepper, finely diced
½ cup (125 mL) chopped cilantro
salt and pepper to taste

DRESSING

9　Combine the garlic, mustard, olive oil, balsamic vinegar
and maple syrup in a jar with a tightly fitting lid and shake
vigorously.

SALAD

10　Place the quinoa in a large bowl. Add the tomatoes,
cucumber, orange pepper, and cilantro. Toss together, add
the dressing, and gently mix in the mussel meat.

MUSSELS ROCKEFELLER

{Serves 6}

MUSSELS

2 lb (1 kg) mussels

¼ cup (60 mL) white wine

½ shallot, diced

TOPPING

2 Tbsp (30 mL) butter

1 garlic clove, minced

1 shallot, diced

3 green onions, chopped

1 rib celery, diced

1 cup (250 mL) baby spinach

½ cup (125 mL) cream (35%)

½ cup (125 mL) dry breadcrumbs

½ cup (125 mL) grated Parmesan
  cheese

6 pitted black olives, sliced

THIS DISH is a variation on the classic Oysters Rockefeller created in New Orleans in 1899. It was named for John D. Rockefeller, the richest man in America at the time. The dish was created as an answer to the shortage of French snails. We have only one question: why not mussels? This recipe can also be served in small individual serving dishes instead of in shells.

MUSSELS

1   Rinse the mussels under running fresh water. Throw away any that do not close.

2   In a large pot, add the wine, shallot and mussels. Cover with a lid and cook on high for approximately 5 to 6 minutes or until steam is pouring out from under the lid.

3   Let the mussels cool. Remove the mussel meat from the shells and put it in a covered bowl or dish. Save the shells.

4   Refrigerate until ready to assemble.

TOPPING

5   Melt the butter in a sauté pan over medium heat. Add the garlic, shallot, green onions and celery, and cook until soft.

6   Toss in the spinach and stir until it is wilted.

7   Add the cream and cook for a few minutes, until the mixture starts to thicken, add the bread crumbs and stir gently.

8 Choose 24 large mussel shells. Break them in half and place the half shells on a baking sheet lined with parchment paper. Add one or two mussels to each shell, then top with the topping, sprinkle with Parmesan cheese and refrigerate until needed.

9 Before serving, bake the mussels in a 350°F (175°C) oven for approximately 5 to 7 minutes or until the cheese starts to bubble and turn golden brown. Top with the olives.

MUSSELS ON THE HALF SHELL

with Blueberry Maple Vinaigrette

{Serves 4}

MUSSELS

1 lb (500 g) mussels

¼ cup (60 mL) white wine

2 green onions, chopped

1 garlic clove, finely chopped

BLUEBERRY MAPLE VINAIGRETTE

½ tsp (2.5 mL) Dijon mustard

½ tsp (2.5 mL) salt

¼ tsp (1 mL) fresh ground black pepper

1 clove of garlic, minced

⅓ cup (80 mL) maple syrup

⅓ cup (80 mL) balsamic vinegar

½ cup (125 mL) blueberry juice

⅔ cup (160 mL) vegetable oil

handful of your favourite fresh herbs, finely chopped

MUSSELS ON THE half shell are a very popular choice for hors d'oeuvres at parties and receptions—they're "finger friendly," easy to pass around and come with their own serving dishes.

MUSSELS

1 Rinse the mussels under running fresh water. Throw away any that do not close.

2 In a large pot, add the wine, onions, garlic and mussels. Cover with a lid and cook on high for approximately 5 to 6 minutes or until steam is pouring out from under the lid.

3 Let the mussels cool. Remove the mussel meat from the shells and put it in a covered bowl or dish.

4 Refrigerate until ready to assemble.

5 Break the shells into halves and place on a serving platter.

VINAIGRETTE

6 Mix together the mustard, salt, pepper and garlic. Add the maple syrup, balsamic vinegar, blueberry juice and oil, and whisk until emulsified. Refrigerate for at least 30 minutes. For best results prepare the vinaigrette the day before.

ASSEMBLY

7 Place a mussel in each half shell, then top with the vinaigrette.

8 Garnish with the herbs.

ASIAN FRESH ROLLS
with Maple Ginger Dipping Sauce
{Serves 12}

MUSSELS
5 lb (2.2 kg) mussels
¼ cup (60 mL) white wine

MAPLE GINGER DIPPING SAUCE
2 Tbsp (30 mL) sesame seeds
1 Tbsp (15 mL) sesame oil
1 clove of garlic, finely chopped
2 Tbsp (30 mL) minced fresh
  ginger
8 tsp (40 mL) Asian-style hot
  chili sauce
½ cup (125 mL) fish sauce
2 cups (500 mL) pure maple
  syrup

Fresh rolls, sometimes referred to as "salad rolls," originated in Vietnam, where they are a popular street food. They typically consist of meat, fish, vegetables, rice noodles and herbs wrapped in rice paper and served with a dipping sauce. Not being deep-fried, they are a healthy alternative to traditional fresh spring rolls. Alain developed this recipe for the first cooking class we did for consumers in Ontario because he was looking for a sweet recipe using fruit.

■   ■

MUSSELS
1   Rinse the mussels under running fresh water. Throw away any that do not close.

2   In a large pot, add the mussels and wine. Cover with a lid and cook on high for approximately 6 to 8 minutes or until steam is pouring out from under the lid.

3   Let the mussels cool. Remove the mussel meat from the shells. Put it in a covered bowl or dish and refrigerate.

MAPLE GINGER DIPPING SAUCE
4   In a saucepan, toast the sesame seeds over medium heat until they become fragrant. Add the sesame oil, garlic and ginger and sauté lightly. Add 2 tsp (10 mL) chili sauce, fish sauce and maple syrup. Bring to a boil, and then reduce to low and allow to simmer for 5 minutes. Cool.

ASSEMBLY

12 medium rice paper wrappers

8 oz (250 g) of rice vermicelli
   noodles, cooked according to
   package directions

½ cup (125 mL) julienne pickled
   daikon

½ cup (125 mL) fresh blueberries

2 Tbsp (30 mL) pickled ginger

12 green onions, green part only

ASSEMBLY

5   Dip the rice paper wrappers one at a time into warm water until just pliable. Place each wrapper on a flat surface in front of you, and put $^1/_{12}$ of the vermicelli noodles vertically in the centre of the wrapper. Add 3 strands of the daikon, 6 to 8 blueberries, 2 to 3 pieces of pickled ginger and 6 to 8 mussels. Finish with ½ tsp (2.5 mL) of chili sauce.

6   Fold in the two ends on your left and right. Lay the green onion on top horizontally so that the end protrudes a couple of inches (5 cm) from the roll. Roll from bottom to top as tightly as possible.

7   Serve with the maple ginger dipping sauce.

MUSSEL LETTUCE WRAP

{Serves 4}

1 head lettuce (bibb or iceberg)

MUSSELS

3 lb (1.5 kg) mussels

½ cup (125 mL) white wine

TERIYAKI

2 Tbsp (30 mL) sesame oil

2 Tbsp (30 mL) teriyaki sauce

2 Tbsp (30 mL) honey

1 Tbsp (15 mL) grated ginger

1 Tbsp (15 mL) soy sauce

1 cup (250 mL) julienne carrots
   (2-inch/5 cm lengths)

1 cup (250 mL) bamboo shoots

1 cup (250 mL) julienne green
   onions (2-inch/5 cm lengths)

½ cup (125 mL) sliced
   mushrooms

1 garlic clove, diced

1 red pepper, seeds and veins
   removed, julienne

1 chili, medium heat, seeds and
   veins removed, diced

½ cup (125 mL) chopped roasted
   peanuts

THIS IS AN Asian-inspired recipe with lots of flavour and an interesting presentation because you use lettuce instead of wheat-based wraps. When Linda lived in Australia, lettuce wraps were frequently offered on Thai menus, and she has adapted the classic method to use mussels. It is a great recipe for those who are also looking for low-carbohydrate recipes but don't want to miss out on any flavours. It has sweet, sour, heat and crunch all in one mouthful.

■   ■

1   Remove the core from the head of lettuce. Pull the leaves apart, wash and leave to dry.

MUSSELS

2   Rinse the mussels under running fresh water. Throw away any that do not close.

3   In a large pot, add the mussels and wine. Cover with a lid and cook on high for approximately 5 to 6 minutes or until steam is pouring out from under the lid.

4   Let the mussels cool. Remove the mussel meat from the shells and put it in a covered bowl or dish.

5   Refrigerate until ready to assemble.

TERIYAKI

6   In a bowl, whisk together half the sesame oil, the teriyaki sauce, honey, ginger and soy sauce. Add the carrots, bamboo shoots and green onions and ensure they are well coated. Set aside.

7   Pour the rest of the sesame oil into a large non-stick frying pan, and on medium heat, add the mushrooms, garlic, pepper and chili. Cook for about 2 to 3 minutes.

8 Add the mussels and the teriyaki mixture containing the carrots, bamboo shoots and green onions. Gently stir until the mixture is heated through. Do not let the vegetables get soft.

ASSEMBLY

9 This is a fun dish to serve family style. Put the lettuce leaves on a big plate and spoon the Asian mussel mixture into a dish with a cover. Sprinkle the nuts overtop and take the lettuce and the mussel mixture to the table. Let everyone fill their own lettuce wraps, roll the leaves up and start nibbling from the end.

MARINATED MUSSELS

{Serves a crowd}

MUSSELS

3 lb (1.5 kg) mussels

¼ cup (60 mL) white wine

MARINADE

your choice of marinade
ingredients (see next page)

HERE ARE A few variations on marinated mussels. They make wonderful appetizers for a crowd: you can make them ahead, and people can compare their favourite flavours. Marinated mussels are very popular in New Zealand and are available commercially at the grocery stores.

MUSSELS

1   Rinse the mussels under running fresh water. Throw away any that do not close.

2   In a large pot, add the mussels and wine. Cover with a lid and cook on high for approximately 5 to 6 minutes or until steam is pouring out from under the lid.

3   Let the mussels cool. Remove the mussel meat from the shells and put it in a covered bowl or dish. If desired, save the shells for serving the mussels.

4   Refrigerate until ready to assemble.

MARINADE

5   In a glass bowl, combine your chosen marinade ingredients.

ASSEMBLY

6   Add the cooked mussel meat to the marinade and toss gently. Cover the bowl with plastic wrap and put in the refrigerator for about 3 to 4 hours. To serve, spoon the mussels into a serving dish, add a bit of the marinade so that they don't dry out, put some toothpicks on the side and let your guests dig in. If you want to get a little fancier, serve each mussel in a half shell. You can also make this recipe a day ahead.

CITRUS MUSSEL MARINADE

juice of 1 lemon

juice of 1 lime

juice of 1 orange

2 Tbsp (30 mL) lemon zest

3 garlic cloves, sliced

1 Tbsp (15 mL) sweet German
   mustard

⅓ cup (80 mL) white sugar

1 sweet onion, cut in half and
   thinly sliced

1 Tbsp (15 mL) vegetable oil

SPICY MUSSEL MARINADE

1 jalapeño chili, seeds removed
   and thinly sliced

¼ cup (60 mL) cider vinegar

¼ cup (60 mL) brown sugar

1 Tbsp (15 mL) mustard seeds

2 cloves garlic, very thinly sliced

2 tsp (10 mL) coriander seeds

1 Tbsp (15 mL) olive oil

THAI MUSSEL MARINADE

⅓ cup (80 mL) rice wine vinegar

juice of 1 lime

2 Tbsp (30 mL) cilantro, finely
   chopped

2 cloves garlic, sliced thinly

⅓ cup (80 mL) white sugar

1 Tbsp (15 mL) canola oil

1 tsp (5 mL) grainy mustard

10 green onions, tops taken off,
   cut in 2-inch (5 cm) pieces on
   the bias

SWEET MUSSEL MARINADE

¼ cup (60 mL) white sugar

½ cup (125 mL) white balsamic
   vinegar

½ sweet onion, finely diced

1 Tbsp (15 mL) honey garlic
   mustard

1 Tbsp (15 mL) olive oil

3 cloves garlic, finely diced

1 tsp (5 mL) celery seeds

1 bay leaf

SHERRY MUSSEL MARINADE

⅓ cup (80 mL) sherry vinegar

⅓ cup (80 mL) brown sugar

½ red pepper, seeded, deveined
   and very thinly sliced

½ green pepper, seeded, deveined
   and very thinly sliced

1 Tbsp (15 mL) capers

1 tsp (5 mL) Dijon mustard

1 Tbsp (15 mL) olive oil

RED WINE MUSSEL MARINADE

½ cup (125 mL) red wine

10 cloves garlic, roasted

¼ cup (60 mL) brown sugar

½ bulb fresh fennel, sliced very
   thinly

2 cinnamon sticks

4 sprigs fresh thyme

1 Tbsp (15 mL) sweet mustard

1 Tbsp (15 mL) olive oil

RED WINE

SPICY

SWEET

CITRUS

THAI

SHERRY

TARANTA PAN-ROASTED MUSSELS

CHEF JOSE DUARTE, TARANTA RESTAURANT, BOSTON, MASSACHUSETTS

{Serves 2}

3 shallots, peeled

1 cup (250 mL) balsamic vinegar

½ cup (125 mL) water

3 Tbsp (45 mL) olive oil

2 oz (60 g) Pancetta, skin removed and chopped

1½ lb (750 g) mussels

¾ cup (185 mL) sweet Marsala or sweet sherry

salt and pepper to taste

2 Tbsp (30 mL) chopped parsley

FOR YEARS JOSE and Alain have been promoting seafood together in the Boston area. A few years ago, Jose visited some mussel farms in PEI and fell in love with both the product and the industry. He has been serving this signature dish in his restaurant ever since. Yes, we got him to share the secret with us.

1 Rinse the mussels under running fresh water. Throw away any that do not close.

2 In a small ovenproof sauté pan, add 1 Tbsp (15 mL) of the olive oil and the shallots, stirring until the whole shallots are golden brown.

3 Add the balsamic vinegar and water, cover with foil and place in the oven for 40 minutes at 350°F (175°C).

4 Remove the shallots and save the vinegar for other uses (in salads, etc.).

5 Heat a sauté pan and add the remaining olive oil and the diced pancetta. After it browns a little, add the shallots and the mussels and toss until the mussels are coated with the oily mix.

6 Deglaze the pan with the Marsala wine. Add salt and pepper, and cover the pan until the mussels are open (4 to 5 minutes).

7 Transfer the broth and shallots into another sauté pan and reduce to a third.

8 Place the mussels on a plate and pour the sauce on top, then sprinkle with the chopped parsley.

COCONUT AND PANKO MUSSELS

{Serves 4}

MUSSELS

3 lb (1.5 kg) mussels

¼ cup (60 mL) white wine

1⅓ cups (335 mL) flour

1 tsp (5 mL) baking powder

¼ tsp (1 mL) baking soda

1 Tbsp (15 mL) sugar

1 large egg, lightly beaten

1½ cups (375 mL) buttermilk

1 Tbsp (15 mL) melted butter

1 cup (250 mL) coconut flakes

¾ cup (185 mL) panko crumbs

4 cups (1 L) vegetable oil

SAUCE

½ cup (125 mL) honey

1 tsp (5 mL) Dijon mustard

½ tsp (2.5 mL) chili flakes

THIS RECIPE WILL satisfy that finger food craving that we all get from time to time. While trying to keep all of our recipes healthy and nutritious, sometimes we think we all need something deep-fried, and this crunchy and wonderfully sweet appetizer will do the trick.

MUSSELS

1 Rinse the mussels under running fresh water. Throw away any that do not close.

2 In a large pot, add the mussels and wine. Cover with a lid and cook on high for approximately 5 to 6 minutes or until steam is pouring out from under the lid.

3 Once the mussels are cool, remove the meat from the shells and refrigerate.

4 In a large bowl, combine the flour, baking powder, baking soda and sugar.

5 In a small bowl, incorporate the beaten egg, buttermilk and melted butter.

6 Make a well in the centre of the dry ingredients, and add the wet ingredients and mix well.

7 In a small bowl, mix the coconut and panko together. Dip the mussels into the batter, and then roll in the coconut and panko mixture. Heat a deep fryer to 350°F (175°C). Drop the mussels into the vegetable oil and fry until the mussels are golden brown. Drain on paper towels.

SAUCE

8 Gently warm the honey over low heat, whisk in the mustard and chili flakes, warm through and serve alongside the

⚓

SWISS-STYLE MUSSELS

CHEF FRANK WIDMER, PARK HYATT IN ZURICH, SWITZERLAND

{Serves 4}

2 sprigs cilantro

2 Tbsp (30 mL) fresh dill

3 Tbsp (45 mL) parsley

½ cup (125 mL) soft butter

¼ cup (60 mL) flour

1¼ cups (310 mL) chopped white
   onion

⅔ cup (160 mL) chopped garlic

8 cups (2 L) apple cider

5 lb (2.2 kg) fresh mussels

2 cups (500 mL) apple juice

salt and pepper to taste

cayenne to taste

4 cups (1 L) cream

FRANK AND ALAIN have been friends for many years and have had the pleasure of cooking together at numerous events. Frank's family-style approach to this dish is true to his warm personality. You can place the pot or the biggest bowl from your kitchen in the middle of the table, and everybody can help themselves. Serve the mussels with fresh baguette and a lovely glass of white wine.

■   ■

1   Wash the cilantro, dill and parsley and let them dry on a cloth. Chop and mix well. Set aside.

2   Work 2 Tbsp (30 mL) of the butter into the flour until you get a smooth dough. Set aside.

3   In a very large pot, melt the rest of the butter on medium heat. Add the onion and the garlic and slowly fry them on low heat, so that they don't change colour, for about 3 minutes (until they have a glassy look).

4   Add half the mixed herbs, stir well, and pour in the cider. Bring to a boil, and then add the mussels to the pot, cover with a lid and steam them on high heat until the mussel shells are open (6 to 8 minutes).

5   Take the steamed mussels out of the broth in the pot (keep the broth in the pan), and place them in a colander to drain.

6   Prepare another pot with a strainer and a piece of cheesecloth placed in the strainer. Pour the broth through the cloth and the strainer (the cloth will hold back the onion, garlic and the herbs).

7   Add the apple juice to the broth and bring to a boil.
    Season with salt and pepper, and then with a whisk, stir
    in flakes of the butter-flour mixture, little by little, until
    the broth has the thickness of a sauce. Let simmer for 20
    minutes.

8   Add the cream to the sauce, check the seasoning one more
    time and add a little cayenne pepper. Bring to a boil, and
    add the rest of the herbs.

9   Wash the first pot, place the mussels in it, pour the hot
    sauce overtop and bring to a boil.

CHORIZO CIDER MUSSELS

{Serves 4}

5 lb (2.2 kg) mussels

1 Tbsp (15 mL) olive oil

¾ cup (185 mL) fresh Spanish
   chorizo sausages, skins removed

1 small onion, finely diced

1 garlic clove, sliced

1 Tbsp (15 mL) chopped rosemary

1 cup (250 mL) apple cider

4 sprigs fresh rosemary, for
   garnish

zest of 1 lemon

CHORIZO SAUSAGES HAVE a smoky flavour and are a deep red colour from the peppers and paprika used to flavour them. You can find them both fresh and cured in your supermarket; however, Alain has used fresh ones in this recipe. We have added some sweetness with the cider to balance the spiciness of the sausages.

1   Rinse the mussels under running fresh water. Throw away any that do not close.

2   Heat the oil in a frying pan over medium heat and cook the sausages for 7 to 8 minutes until brown. Add the onion, garlic and rosemary and stir for a couple of minutes. Add the mussels, and then pour the cider overtop. Cover with a lid and turn the heat up to the highest setting. Cook for about 6 to 8 minutes or until the steam starts to barrel out from under the lid.

3   Spoon into a bowl or bowls, and pour the broth over the mussels. You can add a few sprigs of fresh rosemary and the lemon zest to garnish.

MEDITERRANEAN MUSSELS

{Serves 4}

TOPPING

2 plum tomatoes, seeded and
   finely diced
¼ red onion, diced
12 pitted kalamata olives,
   chopped
juice and zest of 1 lemon
¼ cup (60 mL) olive oil
1 sprig of thyme, stem removed
1 Tbsp (15 mL) chopped parsley
1 tsp (5 mL) oregano
salt and pepper to taste

MUSSELS

2 lb (1 kg) mussels
¼ cup (60 mL) white wine
juice of half a lemon

ASSEMBLY

¼ cup (60 mL) crumbled feta

THIS IS THE perfect choice for a canapé reception. The Mediterranean flavours are vibrant, fresh and a real crowd-pleaser.

TOPPING

1 Incorporate the tomatoes, onions, olives, lemon zest and juice, olive oil, thyme, parsley and oregano in a large bowl. Toss and then finish with salt and pepper. Refrigerate.

MUSSELS

2 Rinse the mussels under running fresh water. Throw away any that do not close.

3 In a large pot, add the mussels, wine and lemon juice. Cover with a lid and cook on high for approximately 5 to 6 minutes or until steam is pouring out from under the lid.

4 Let the mussels cool. Remove the mussel meat from the shells and put it in a covered bowl or dish. Reserve half the shells.

5 Refrigerate until ready to assemble.

ASSEMBLY

6 Preheat the oven to 350°F (175°C)

7 Choose 24 shells and break them in half. Place the half shells on a baking sheet and place one or two mussels in each shell.

8 Using a teaspoon, fill each shell with the tomato mixture.

9 Finish with the crumbled feta and bake in the oven for 10 minutes.

Chapter 2

THE SOUPS, STEWS 'N' CHOWDERS

TOM KHA SOUP
with Mussels
{Serves 4}

BROTH

5 lb (2.2 kg) mussels

½ cup (125 mL) white wine

¼ cup (60 mL) shallots

¼ cup (60 mL) cilantro

2 stalks of lemon grass (use the back of a knife to bruise the stalks)

2 lime leaves

one 14 oz (398 mL) can coconut milk

1 tsp (5 mL) salt

1 tsp (5 mL) ground pepper

ACCOMPANIMENTS

4 oz (125 g) rice vermicelli noodles, cooked according to the instructions on the package

6 sprigs cilantro

1 cup (250 mL) spinach leaves

1 cup (250 mL) sliced mushrooms

1 red pepper, sliced

one 14 oz (398 mL) can baby corn, rinsed and drained

Sriracha sauce

IF YOU'VE NEVER tried Tom Kha soup, you're missing out. The coconut milk makes it velvety and smooth, and the lemon grass and lime give it the slightest hint of tanginess. We've added a very social aspect to this version by making the broth ahead and allowing the guests to assemble the soup individually.

BROTH

1   Rinse the mussels under running fresh water. Throw away any that do not close.

2   Place the mussels, wine, shallots, cilantro, crushed lemon grass, and lime leaves into a large pot. Cover and place over high heat, then steam for 6 to 8 minutes until steam pours out from under the lid.

3   Remove the mussels and set aside to cool.

4   Turn the heat to high and bring the broth back to a boil, reduce the heat to medium and stir in the coconut milk, salt and pepper.

5   Remove the meat from the mussels and add it back to the broth, allow it to heat through.

ACCOMPANIMENTS

6   To serve, lay out the spinach, mushrooms, peppers and baby corn buffet-style for your guests.

7   Have them place a preferred selection of ingredients into their bowls, and then ladle the hot broth on top.

8   Serve with Chinese spoons and chopsticks.

⚓ MUSSEL CHOWDER
with Brie and Basil
{Serves 6}

MUSSELS
2 lb (1 kg) mussels

¾ cup (185 mL) white wine

CHOWDER
1 lb (500 g) yellow flesh
  potatoes, skin on, diced

4 cups (1 L) water

2 shallots, diced

2 Tbsp (30 mL) butter

4 slices bacon, finely diced

½ cup (125 mL) diced celery

1 Tbsp (15 mL) Dijon mustard

2 Tbsp (30 mL) chopped fresh
  basil

2 bay leaves

1 small wheel of double cream
  brie, sliced

1 cup (250 mL) cream (35%)

salt and pepper to taste

IN THE MARITIMES, everyone has their own seafood chowder recipe. They are closely guarded secrets handed down throughout the generations like family jewels. Now you have one too—and it's gluten-free, as it uses potatoes to thicken the chowder.

■　　　　　　■

MUSSELS

1   Rinse the mussels under running fresh water. Throw away any that do not close.

2   In a large pot, add the mussels and ½ cup (125 mL) of the white wine. Cover with a lid and cook on high for approximately 5 to 6 minutes or until steam is pouring out from under the lid.

3   Let the mussels cool. Remove the mussel meat from the shells and put it in a covered bowl or dish. Reserve 4 cups (1 L) of the broth.

4   Refrigerate the mussel meat and broth until ready to assemble.

CHOWDER

5   Boil half the potatoes and half the shallots in 4 cups (1 L) of water until tender. Purée and set aside.

6   In a large pot, sauté the bacon, the remaining shallots and the celery in the butter until transparent, then deglaze with the remaining white wine and Dijon mustard. When the wine has reduced by half, add the remaining potatoes, the herbs and the reserved mussel broth. Bring to a boil and then reduce the heat to a gentle simmer until the potatoes are just fork-tender.

7   When the potatoes are cooked, add the mussel meat, brie and the puréed potato, and cook for a further five minutes. Season with salt and pepper, stir in the cream and allow to heat through. Adjust the seasoning to taste.

MUSSEL BOUILLABAISSE

{Serves 4}

2 Tbsp (30 mL) olive oil

2 garlic cloves, minced

2 medium carrots, diced

½ bulb fennel, julienne

2 celery ribs, diced

2 bay leaves

1 tsp (5 mL) chili powder

6 threads of saffron

½ cup (125 mL) white wine

one 28 oz (796 mL) can diced
  tomatoes with liquid

2 lb (1 kg) mussels

BOUILLABAISSE, OR FISHERMEN'S stew, originated in the Provence region of France in the city of Marseilles. What made it unique to the region was the blend of Provençal herbs and spices used in the broth. These days, there are as many different versions of bouillabaisse as there are fish in the sea.

1   Heat the olive oil in a large pot over medium heat. Sauté the garlic, carrots, fennel and celery until translucent.

2   Add the bay leaves, chili powder and saffron, and stir until the spices become fragrant.

3   Deglaze the pot with the white wine. Add the tomatoes and bring to a boil. Reduce to a simmer, and cook until the vegetables are tender, approximately 20 minutes.

4   Rinse the mussels under running fresh water. Throw away any that do not close.

5   Add the mussels to the pot, cover and cook on high heat for 5 to 6 minutes or until steam is pouring out from under the lid.

6   Ladle into large bowls and serve with crusty bread.

7   To create a seafood bouillabaisse, add extra seafood when you add the mussels.

⚓

MUSSEL BISQUE
{Serves 4}

4 lb (1.8 kg) mussels

½ cup (125 mL) white wine

½ cup (125 mL) diced leeks, white
  part only

½ cup (125 mL) butter

½ cup (125 mL) finely diced
  carrot

½ cup (125 mL) finely diced
  celery

3 Tbsp (45 mL) chopped fresh
  dill

3 Tbsp (45 mL) chopped fresh
  basil

3 tomatoes, seeded and diced

½ cup (125 mL) converted rice

1 cup (250 mL) cream (35%)

2 cups (500 mL) cream (10%)

6 threads saffron

To call this a true bisque would be a bit misleading, as authentic bisque uses the bodies of the shellfish by roasting or simmering them instead of steaming them. However, it does have many of the same elements such as the rich, smooth creaminess. Using rice as a thickener is very traditional in bisques. This recipe calls for using an immersion blender. If you don't have one, you can also use a regular blender or food processor.

■　　　　　　　　　　　■

1　Rinse the mussels under running fresh water. Throw away any that do not close.

2　In a large pot, add the wine, one quarter of the leeks, and the mussels. Cover with a lid and cook on high for approximately 6 to 8 minutes or until steam is pouring out from under the lid.

3　Once the mussels are cool, remove the meat from the shells, place in a covered dish and refrigerate. Reserve 6 cups (1.5 L) of the broth.

4　Melt the butter in a large stock pot. When it just begins to brown, add the carrots, celery, dill, basil and the remainder of the leeks and and sauté until soft.

5　Add the tomatoes, the reserved mussel broth and rice. Bring to a boil, and then lower the heat and simmer for an hour.

6　Purée using an immersion blender. Add the saffron and both the 35% and 10% cream, let simmer for another 10 minutes, then stir in the mussel meat. Serve in individual bowls.

MUSSEL, BACON AND CORN CHOWDER

{Serves 4}

3 lb (1.5 kg) mussels

½ cup (125 mL) white wine

2 Tbsp (30 mL) olive oil

8 slices double smoked bacon,
  finely diced

1 cup (250 mL) sweet onion,
  diced

1 cup (250 mL) corn kernels

2 celery ribs, diced

4 cups (1 L) mussel broth

3 cups (750 mL) potatoes, diced

3 Tbsp (45 mL) flour

one 14 oz (398 mL) can
  evaporated milk

salt and pepper to taste

THIS IS AN old-fashioned type of chowder, and for Alain, it's all about the evaporated milk, which makes it comforting. Maritime kitchens would always have a can of evaporated milk on hand for the tea.

■ ■

1 Rinse the mussels under running fresh water. Throw away any that do not close.

2 In a large pot, add the mussels and wine. Cover with a lid and cook on high for approximately 5 to 6 minutes or until steam is pouring out from under the lid.

3 Let the mussels cool. Remove the mussel meat from the shells and put it in a covered bowl or dish. Discard the shells.

4 Reserve 4 cups (1 L) of the broth. Refrigerate until ready to assemble.

5 Heat the olive oil in a medium-sized pot. Sauté the bacon until crisp, and then remove and set aside. Sauté the onions, corn and celery in the remaining bacon fat until tender, add the mussel broth and potatoes and bring to a boil. Reduce the heat and simmer for 15 minutes.

6 Make a paste with the flour and ¼ cup (60 mL) of the evaporated milk. Gradually stir the remaining milk into the potato mixture. Drop in the flour paste and stir until well blended. Heat until thickened.

7 Gently stir in the mussels and the reserved bacon and allow them to heat through. Add salt and pepper.

CURRY SEAFOOD MUSSEL CHOWDER

{Serves 4}

6 slices pancetta, diced

½ cup (125 mL) diced green or
   red pepper

½ cup (125 mL) sweet white
   onion

½ cup (125 mL) finely diced
   celery

5 lb (2.2 kg) mussels

½ cup (125 mL) white wine

2 cups (500 mL) cream (10%)

8 oz (250 g) canned crabmeat

1½ cups (375 mL) diced cooked
   potatoes

2 Tbsp (30 mL) curry powder

1 lb (500 g) raw white fish, cut
   into 1-inch (2.5 cm) pieces

1 cup (250 mL) raw scallops

1 cup (250 mL) peeled shrimp

1 tsp (5 mL) cornstarch

¼ cup (60 mL) milk

2 Tbsp (30 mL) finely chopped
   chives

salt and pepper to taste

LINDA THINKS MUSSELS make the best broth ever and are the perfect base for chowder. She visited Eric Ripert's restaurant, Le Bernadin, in New York City a few years ago and could not understand why they needed so many mussels for the promotional lunch she was hosting for major magazine food editors and their chefs. When she went into the kitchen to inquire, the reply was simple: "For the broth, Madame, for the broth!" They used the mussel broth for many of their signature fish sauces and soups. She likes to make this chowder, cool it and put it into the refrigerator for 12 to 24 hours. This give more time for the flavours to blend, and she thinks it makes for a tastier chowder. Just reheat on low to medium when you are ready to serve it.

■   ■

1   Rinse the mussels under running fresh water. Throw away any that do not close.

2   In a large pot, add the pancetta and stir for 1 to 2 minutes. Add the peppers, onion and celery and sauté until they are soft.

3   Pour the mussels and wine into the pot, cover with a lid and turn the heat up to the highest setting on your stove. Cook for 6 to 8 minutes or until steam is pouring out from under the lid.

4   With a large slotted spoon, remove the mussels from the pot.

5   Shuck the meat from the shells, and put the mussel meat back in the pot with the broth. Discard the shells, unless you want to save a few for a nice presentation in your chowder bowls.

6   Slowly add the cream, crab, potatoes and curry powder
    to the broth, and cook on medium heat. Drop the fish
    and scallops into the chowder and cook for another
    10 minutes. Add the shrimp.

7   In a small bowl, mix the cornstarch and milk together,
    and slowly whisk into the chowder. Cook for another
    5 minutes.

8   Ladle into bowls and finish with the chives. Season with
    salt and pepper.

CREAMY MUSSEL SOUP

{Serves 6}

BROTH

5 lb (2.2 kg) mussels

1 Tbsp (15 mL) butter

2 bunches green onion, whites
   only, sliced thin

1 bay leaf

2 sprigs fresh thyme

½ cup (125 mL) white wine

This recipe is Linda's variation on the famous Billi Bi Soup. There are a number of theories about where it came from: some believe it came from the Brittany coast, others claim a chef at Maxim's of Paris named it after his customer William B. (Billy B.) Leeds, an American tin tycoon. It is rich and silky, and the flavour will ward off any feelings of guilt about the cream once you have tasted it.

■ ■

BROTH

1   Rinse the mussels under running fresh water. Throw away any that do not close.

2   In a large pot, melt the butter. Add green onions, bay leaf and thyme, and stir until they have softened.

3   Pour the mussels and wine into the pot, cover with a lid and turn the heat up to the highest setting on your stove. Cook for 6 to 8 minutes or until steam is pouring out from under the lid.

4   With a large slotted spoon, remove the mussels. Reserve 24 mussels with the meat inside, and shuck the rest. Strain the broth with cheesecloth or a very fine sieve. Some people like to add the shucked mussel meat to the soup later. If you do this, add the mussel meat to the broth to heat it before serving. The mussel meat can also be used for other recipes.

SOUP

2 cups (500 mL) cream (35%)
1 egg yolk, lightly beaten
dash of paprika

SOUP

5   Return the broth to the pot on medium heat, and slowly add the cream. After it is heated, temper the egg yolk by ladling some of the hot broth into a small bowl, slowly add the egg yolk while whisking vigorously, and return it to the pot. Cook for about 10 minutes, stirring to ensure it doesn't stick to the bottom.

6   In each soup bowl, ladle some soup, and add 4 mussels in their shells. Finish with a dash of paprika.

CAJUN MUSSEL SOUP

{Serves 4}

2 lb (1 kg) mussels

¼ cup (60 mL) white wine

2 Tbsp (30 mL) butter

¼ cup (60 mL) chopped onion

2 Tbsp (30 mL) flour

¼ cup (60 mL) chopped celery

¼ cup (60 mL) chopped carrot

1 green onion, chopped

1 Tbsp (15 mL) tomato paste

1 garlic clove, minced

2 tsp (10 mL) Cajun seasoning

2 drops hot sauce

½ lb (250 g) white fish, cut into
   1½-inch (4 cm) pieces

½ cup (125 mL) cream (35%)

salt and pepper to taste

THIS RECIPE EVOLVED out of Alain's desire to recreate the amazing flavours he found while he was in Louisiana. The food in New Orleans is brimming with flavours that are so simple, yet so complex at the same time. Cajun food has become one of his favourite styles of cooking.

1   Rinse the mussels under running fresh water. Throw away any that do not close.

2   In a large pot, add mussels and wine. Cover with a lid and cook on high for approximately 5 to 6 minutes or until steam is pouring out from under the lid.

3   Let the mussels cool. Remove the mussel meat from the shells and put it in a covered bowl or dish. Reserve 2 cups (500 mL) of the broth.

4   Melt the butter in a medium-sized stock pot over medium heat. Sauté the onions until they are golden brown.

5   Sprinkle the flour over the butter and whisk gently to make a paste. You want to cook the flour to remove the raw taste without letting it burn.

6   When the flour has turned a golden brown, begin gradually adding the mussel broth, stirring constantly as it thickens.

7   Add the celery, carrot, green onion, tomato paste, garlic, Cajun seasoning, hot sauce and fish; bring to a boil, then lower the heat and simmer for half an hour or until the vegetables are cooked, stirring occasionally.

8   Add the mussel meat and finish with the cream and salt and pepper.

NOODLE BOWLS

{Serves 2}

2 lb (1 kg) mussels

2 portobello mushrooms

1 Tbsp (15 mL) butter

1 garlic clove, diced

¼ cup (60 mL) chopped leeks,
    white part only

½ cup (125 mL) ground pork

½ cup (125 mL) white wine

4 oz (125 g) rice vermicelli
    noodles, cooked according to
    the instructions on the package

2 heads baby bok choy, cut
    lengthwise into quarters

1 cup (250 mL) bean sprouts

¼ cup (60 mL) cashew pieces

2 tsp (10 mL) black bean sauce

Sriracha sauce

THE INSPIRATION FOR this dish is one of Alain's favourite foods, Vietnamese pho soup, a classic street food. He decided to make it less of a soup and more focused on the noodles, so this recipe has less broth than a pho, but it still has that ethnic feel to it.

1   Rinse the mussels under running fresh water. Throw away any that do not close.

2   Cut the mushrooms in half and then slice into ¼ inch (6 mm) slices. In a medium-sized stock pot, melt the butter. Add the garlic and leeks and sauté until soft. Add the ground pork and mushrooms and stir occasionally for 3 to 4 minutes until the pork is no longer pink.

3   Add the mussels and wine. Cover and cook for 6 to 8 minutes or until the mussels open. With a slotted spoon, remove the mussel. Cool and take the mussel meat out of the shells. Set the shells aside.

4   Add the vermicelli noodles and bok choy to the pot and steam for 4 to 6 minutes or until the noodles are cooked and the bok choy is soft.

5   Divide the noodles and the remaining broth between two bowls. Top with the mussel meat, bean sprouts and chopped cashews.

6   Serve with black bean paste and Sriracha.

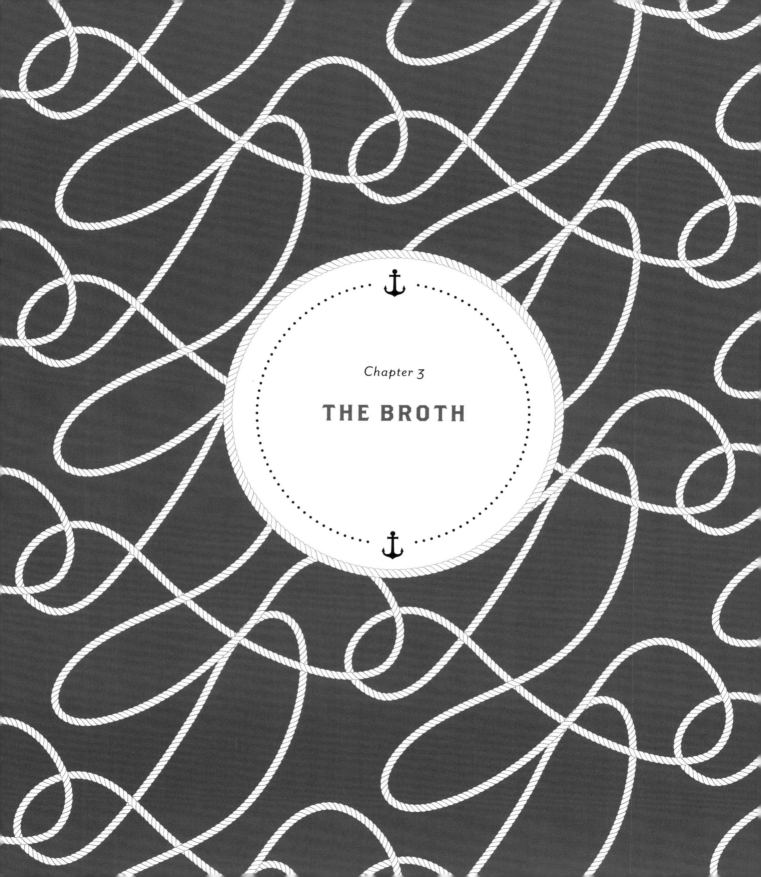

Chapter 3

THE BROTH

THE MUSSEL BROTH

"The best part is the broth!"
—Alain

ALAIN HAS OFTEN said that the broth is the best part of the mussel. He may be kidding, or he may not—that's his secret to keep. Many people, including some of the mussel farmers he knows, disagree with his theory, but the statement always starts a great debate, and that's half the fun!

Alain always drinks any leftover broth or soaks it up with some fresh crusty bread. The thing he loves about mussel broth is its versatility. What you create, and how you use it, is limited only by your imagination. Alain adds it to soups, chowders, sauces, seafood casseroles and risotto. He uses it in cocktails. He poaches fish in it. Freeze any leftover broth in Ziploc bags. You can lay them flat in the freezer so that they take up very little room and are stackable. You will always have broth on hand.

Alain has often referred to mussels as tiny flavour sponges. Mussels will soak up any flavouring that you add to the pot, so keep this in mind when cooking, If you're preparing mussels as an appetizer on Friday and you know that the leftovers will go into a chowder on Saturday, consider adding flavours to the mussel pot that will complement that chowder—flavours such as bacon, tarragon and shallots. Friday's mussels will taste amazing, and the remainder will bring a wallop of added flavour to Saturday's meal.

⚓ GIN MUSSEL SHOOTERS

{Serves 12}

1 lb (500 g) mussels

1 Tbsp (15 mL) butter

¼ cup (60 mL) shallots, chopped

1 medium tomato, diced

½ tsp (2.5 mL) smoked paprika

½ tsp (2.5 mL) dried oregano

4 oz (120 mL) gin

THESE SHOOTERS ARE meant to be served at an hors d'oeuvres party or cocktail reception. Although much of the alcohol cooks out of the gin, Alain still prefers, as a courtesy, to let his guests know that it is an ingredient.

■   ■

1   Rinse the mussels under running fresh water. Throw away any that do not close.

2   Melt the butter in a pot over medium heat. Sauté the shallots, tomato, paprika and oregano until the shallots are translucent.

3   Add the mussels and toss gently, top with the gin, cover and steam over high heat for 4 to 5 minutes or until steam is pouring out from under the lid.

4   Remove the mussel meat, break the shells in half and place the halves on a serving platter. Place two mussels on each half shell, and then top with the broth.

5   Refrigerate, and serve cold.

MUSSEL MAMA COCKTAIL

{Serves 1}

pepper and salt on a side plate

1 lb (500 g) mussels

2 oz (60 mL) white wine

1 lemon wedge

2 oz (60 mL) vodka

8 drops Worcestershire sauce

4 drops Tabasco

1 tsp (5 mL) horseradish

¾ cup (185 mL) vegetable juice

2 pickled asparagus spears, for
   garnish

1 lemon slice, for garnish

HAVE YOU EVER noticed that the ingredients that make a classic Bloody Mary so fantastic are the same ingredients often found in mussel recipes? Well, now you know, so give this cocktail a try. And as you raise your glass, exclaim "Sociable!"—a Maritime tradition much like saying "Cheers."

■   ■

1   Rinse the mussels under running fresh water. Throw away any that do not close.

2   In a large pot, add the mussels and wine. Cover with a lid and cook on high for approximately 5 to 6 minutes or until steam is pouring out from under the lid.

3   Let the mussels cool. Remove the mussel meat from the shells and put it in a covered bowl or dish. Reserve ¼ cup (60 mL) the broth.

4   Take a large 16 oz (475 mL) canning (Mason) jar or a large glass and run a lemon wedge around the rim. Dip in the pepper and salt, and shake off the excess. Fill the jar or glass with ice and put in two ounces (60 mL) of vodka. Add the Worcestershire, tabasco and horseradish to taste. The more you add, the spicier the cocktail will become. Top with the reserved mussel broth and vegetable juice and stir well.

5   Spear 4 mussels on a bamboo stick.

6   Garnish with the mussel skewer, 2 pickled asparagus spears and a lemon slice.

MUSSEL MARTINI
{Serves 1}

1 lb (500 g) mussels
⅛ cup (30 mL) white wine
1 oz (30 mL) vodka
½ oz (15 mL) Limoncello
2 drops of vermouth
1 squeeze of lime
pinch of salt

THIS IDEA POPPED into Alain's head one evening after he overheard someone in his local pub ordering a dirty martini. A dirty martini is made with olive juice. All of a sudden, he had a vision of a martini made with mussels and mussel broth.

■ ■

1   Rinse the mussels under running fresh water. Throw away any that do not close.

2   In a large pot, add the mussels and wine. Cover with a lid and cook on high for approximately 5 to 6 minutes or until steam is pouring out from under the lid.

3   Let the mussels cool. Remove the mussel meat from the shells and put it in a covered bowl or dish. Reserve ¼ cup (60 mL) of the broth and 4 mussels.

4   Fill a cocktail shaker with fresh crushed ice. Add the vodka, Limoncello, vermouth, a quarter cup (60 mL) of the reserved mussel broth, and lime. Shake well; strain and pour into a chilled martini glass and add a pinch of salt.

5   Spear 4 mussels on a bamboo stick and use as a garnish.

GAZPACHO MUSSEL SHOOTERS

{Serves 24 as an hors d'oeuvre or 4 as a soup}

2 lb (1 kg) mussels

¼ cup (60 mL) white wine

2 Roma tomatoes, seeded and
    finely diced

½ medium yellow pepper,
    finely diced

½ English cucumber, finely diced

2 shallots, finely diced

2 ribs celery, finely diced

¼ cup (60 mL) olive oil

1 cup (250 mL) tomato juice

2 Tbsp (30 mL) chipotle
    Tabasco sauce

salt and pepper to taste

THIS WAS A recipe that Alain developed for *Saltscapes* magazine, a lifestyle magazine in Atlantic Canada. Gazpacho is a fresh vegetable soup that is usually served cold and is especially refreshing during the hot summer months. Mussels were the perfect marriage. He invented this shooter style to pass as an hors d'oeuvre, but it can also be served as a soup at a sit-down affair.

1   Rinse the mussels under running fresh water. Throw away any that do not close.

2   In a large pot, add the mussels and wine. Cover with a lid and cook on high for approximately 5 to 6 minutes or until steam is pouring out from under the lid.

3   Let the mussels cool. Remove the mussel meat from the shells and put it in a covered bowl or dish. Reserve 1 cup (250 mL) of the broth. Refrigerate until ready to assemble.

4   Place the tomatoes, peppers, cucumber, shallots and celery in a large bowl. Add the olive oil, mussel broth, tomato juice and Tabasco. Stir well and season with salt and pepper. Refrigerate the gazpacho for at least two hours before serving.

5   To serve, put two mussels in the bottom of each 2 oz (60 mL) shot glass, fill with gazpacho, garnish with an additional mussel and a sprinkle of salt.

6   If serving in bowls, simply add the mussel meat to the soup before serving.

Chapter 4

THE MAINS

SIMPLE STEAMED MUSSELS

{Serves 2}

2 lb (1 kg) mussels

¼ cup (60 mL) white wine

2 green onions, chopped

2 cloves garlic, finely chopped

1 lemon, cut in quarters

¼ cup (50 mL) melted butter

THIS BOOK SHOWS just how versatile mussels really are and how well they adapt to almost any flavour that you choose to pair them with, but both Linda and Alain still enjoy this classic way of preparing mussels above all others. Sometimes simple is best, and a little can go a long way.

1   Rinse the mussels under running fresh water. Throw away any that do not close.

2   In a large pot, add the wine, onions, garlic and mussels. Squeeze ¼ of the lemon over the mussels and add the rind. Cover with a lid and cook on high for approximately 5 to 6 minutes or until steam is pouring out from under the lid.

3   Spoon into a large bowl and serve with crusty bread.

4   Serve the mussels with melted butter for dipping. Any leftover broth can be frozen and used in chowders or other recipes.

BISTRO-STYLE MOULES FRITES

{Serves 4}

FRITES

2 lb (1 kg) russet potatoes

6 cups (1.5 L) canola or
    sunflower oil

salt and pepper to taste

INGREDIENTS CONTINUE...

So HERE WE have it. Here are the two recipes that are used in French bistros around the world to serve you *moules frites*.

Moules marinières is the grandmother of all mussel dishes. It holds its place as a classic French dish, and rightfully so. Like many old recipes, there are numerous versions, but all have the same key ingredients: mussels and potatoes. Some recipes call for a roux or adding a slab of butter or a little cream at the end, but it has such scrumptious flavour that you don't need to add anything else.

Do you like golden crispy french fries? It only takes two ingredients: potatoes and fat. Some people blanch the cut potatoes and cool them before frying, but there is no secret about how to cook potatoes to get a crispy crunch on the outside of the fry—you double-fry them. When Linda lived in England, one of her local pubs triple-fried the potatoes. That's taking it a bit too far, but it looks good on the menu and they were super crunchy!

■ ■

FRITES

1   Wash the potatoes and cut off the two ends. Put the potato on one end and slice downward multiple times until you have about 10 to 12 square fries. Put these into a bowl of cold water as you go so they don't brown while you cut the rest of the potatoes.

2   Heat the oil in a large pan or deep-fryer to about 325°F (160°C).

METHOD CONTINUES...

MOULES

4 lb (1.8 kg) mussels

1 Tbsp (15 mL) butter

1 tsp (5 mL) olive oil

1 small onion, finely diced

1 garlic clove, finely diced

⅛ cup (30 mL) finely diced celery

½ cup (125 mL) white wine

2 Tbsp (30 mL) chopped fresh
   parsley

3   Pull about a quarter of the potatoes out of the cold water and dry them with paper towel. Drop into the oil for about 5 minutes, making sure they don't clump together. When they are just starting to turn golden, remove with a slotted spoon and put on a rack over paper towel to allow the excess oil to drip off.

4   After you have cooked all 4 batches, increase the oil temperature to 350°F (175°C). Depending on the size of your pot, you should be able to double-fry the potatoes in two or three batches.

5   After the first batch is cooked, put it in an ovenproof dish in your oven at 200°F (95°C) to keep warm and crisp until you have finished the final batch. Season with salt and pepper.

MOULES

6   Rinse the mussels under running fresh water. Throw away any that do not close.

7   In a saucepan, melt the butter and oil. Add the onion, garlic and celery and stir for 1 to 2 minutes. Add the mussels and wine and cover with a lid. Turn the heat up to the highest setting. The mussels are ready after about 6 to 8 minutes or when the steam starts to pour out from under the lid.

8   Spoon into bowls and pour the broth over the mussels. Sprinkle the parsley overtop and serve with a plate of the frites.

SWEET THAI CHILI MUSSELS

{Serves 2}

2 lb (1 kg) mussels

¼ cup (60 mL) white wine

1 tsp (5 mL) red onion,
  finely chopped

4 Tbsp (60 mL) sweet Thai
  chili sauce

2 sprigs cilantro, torn

1 lime

THIS RECIPE WAS developed for use at consumer trade shows to show people the amazing versatility of mussels. Thai flavours are popular, and this recipe is no exception. It's simple to prepare but delightfully flavourful and has proved to be a big hit for the tens of thousands of people who have tasted the samples we have been serving over the years!

■ ■

1   Rinse the mussels under running fresh water. Throw away any that do not close.

2   In a large pot, add mussels, wine, onions, chili sauce and cilantro. Cut the lime in half, squeeze the juice over the mussels, and add the rind to the pot. Cover with a lid and cook on high for approximately 5 to 6 minutes or until steam is pouring out from under the lid. Remember to shake the pot occasionally during cooking to make sure the sweet Thai chili sauce coats all the mussels.

3   Serve mussels and sauce in large bowls with your favourite bread for collecting the delicious broth.

SASSY CURRIED MUSSELS

{Serves 2}

2 lb (1 kg) mussels

¼ cup (60 mL) white wine

2 tsp (10 mL) garlic, finely
   chopped

2 green onions, diced

1 rib of celery, finely diced

1 peeled carrot, finely diced

2 tsp (10 mL) curry paste or 1 tsp
   (5 mL) yellow curry powder

¾ cup (185 mL) cream (35%)

CURRY IS ONE of Alain's favourite spices. It's just so warming and soothing that he feels it's the perfect accompaniment to mussels. The cream smoothes it out and gives it a velvety texture that is very pleasing to the palate. Be sure to add lots of sauce to the bowl when serving, and you'll need some good crusty bread for dipping!

1   Rinse the mussels under running fresh water. Throw away any that do not close.

2   In a large pot, add the mussels, wine, garlic, green onion, celery and carrot. Cover with a lid and cook on high for approximately 5 to 6 minutes or until steam is pouring out from under the lid.

3   Remove from the heat and drain away half of the broth. Add the curry and cream and stir well. Cover and return to heat and steam for another 3 to 4 minutes or until the mussels have opened.

4   Transfer the mussels into two large bowls and reduce the sauce, allowing it to thicken slightly. Pour the sauce over the mussels and serve with your favourite bread.

CANADIAN CURRIED MUSSELS

{Serves 2}

2 lb (1 kg) mussels

¼ cup (60 mL) white wine

¼ cup (60 mL) finely chopped
shallots

¼ cup (60 mL) diced red pepper

½ cup (125 mL) maple syrup

1 tsp (5 mL) yellow curry powder

½ cup (125 mL) cream (35%)

THIS RECIPE IS similar to Sassy Curried Mussels (page 103) but with the silky sweetness of pure maple syrup, you get a real Canadian experience. Alain highly recommends using pure maple syrup here as opposed to commercial table syrup if at all possible. One of the top pieces of advice he gives is to always cook with the absolute best ingredients you can afford. It makes a world of difference.

1   Rinse the mussels under running fresh water. Throw away any that do not close.

2   In a large pot, add the mussels, wine, shallots and red pepper. Cover with a lid and cook on high for approximately 5 to 6 minutes or until steam is pouring out from under the lid.

3   Remove the mussels from the broth, cover and set aside.

4   Add the maple syrup and the yellow curry to the broth, bring to a boil and then reduce the heat and simmer for approximately 5 minutes. Add the cream and allow to reduce for another 3 to 4 minutes or until the sauce thickens and coats the back of a spoon.

5   Reintroduce the mussels to the pot and gently mix in with the sauce.

6   Serve with your favourite bread for dipping.

THAI MUSSELS
with Asian Noodles
{Serves 4}

3 lb (1.8 kg) mussels

1 tsp (5 mL) vegetable oil

1 onion, chopped

3 cloves garlic, sliced

1 Tbsp (15 mL) finely diced
  candied ginger

3 tsp (15 mL) green curry paste
  (add a little more if you like your
  curry hotter)

1 tsp (5 mL) fish sauce

½ lime, cut into quarters

1 cup (250 mL) coconut milk

2 Tbsp (30 mL) chopped
  Thai basil

16 oz (875 g) rice vermicelli
  noodles

THAI FOOD HAS become very fashionable in the last decade. People who want to cook with these flavours at home have found that green curry, which has a lot of the same ingredients regardless of the protein you are using, is a tasty and versatile dish to prepare. The sweet and salt characteristics of mussels blend well with this Thai dish, which is known to be sour, sweet, salty and umami.

1   Rinse the mussels under running fresh water. Throw away any that do not close.

2   In a large pot, heat the oil. When hot, add the onion, garlic, candied ginger, curry paste and fish sauce. Stir for two minutes, and then pour in the mussels. Squeeze the lime quarters over the top and toss the rinds into the pot.

3   After 4 minutes, pour the coconut milk over the mussels and sprinkle the basil overtop. Cover with a lid and cook on medium-high for another 4 to 5 minutes until steam is pouring out from under the lid.

4   While the mussels are cooking, heat some water in another pot. Once it boils, add the vermicelli noodles. Stir to loosen the strands, take off the heat and set aside. Keep covered.

5   Once the mussels are cooked, remove from the heat. Stir the mussels to coat all of them with the broth at the bottom.

6   Drain the noodles and divide equally between the bowls. Spoon the mussels on top and then top with the coconut broth. The aroma and taste will be delightful. You may have to sample a few mussels before you put them into the serving bowls. Enjoy.

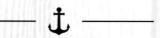

Double-Smoked Bacon and
TARRAGON MUSSELS
{Serves 4}

5 lb (2.2 kg) mussels

⅓ cup (80 mL) diced double-smoked bacon

1 Tbsp (15 mL) finely chopped shallots

2 Tbsp (30 mL) chopped fresh tarragon

¼ cup (60 mL) white wine

½ cup (125 mL) cream (35%)

½ cup (125 mL) arugula

I PREFER DOUBLE-SMOKED bacon because it is smoked up to four times longer than regular bacon. It is cured with a blend of spices in its own juices, so it has a much more complex flavour than regular bacon, with a wonderful rich smokiness.

1   Rinse the mussels under running fresh water. Throw away any that do not close.

2   Sauté the bacon and shallots in a large pot over medium heat, stirring continuously. As soon as the bacon and shallots begin to caramelize, add the tarragon and stir until fragrant.

3   Deglaze the pan with the white wine. Add the mussels and mix. Cover the pot, turn the heat to high and steam for 5 to 6 minutes or until steam is pouring out from under the lid.

4   Using a slotted spoon, remove the mussels from the pot, cover to keep warm, and set aside.

5   Add the cream to the broth and reduce by one quarter.

6   Spoon the mussels into 4 bowls and pour the sauce overtop. Garnish with arugula.

7   Serve with your favourite bread for dipping.

MUSSEL POTATO CAKES

with Apple Chutney

{Serves 4}

APPLE CHUTNEY

2 medium apples

1½ Tbsp (22.5 mL) butter

¼ cup (60 mL) packed brown
  sugar

¼ tsp (1 mL) cinnamon

MUSSEL POTATO CAKES

½ cup (125 mL) apple juice

2 lb (1 kg) mussels

1 large onion, chopped

3 cups (750 mL) cooked mashed
  potatoes

2 Tbsp (30 mL) chopped fresh
  parsley

1½ Tbsp (22.5 mL) summer
  savory

2 eggs, beaten

¼ cup (60 mL) flour

2 Tbsp (30 mL) butter

FISH CAKES ARE a staple in the Maritime provinces. Traditionally they were made with salt cod, but now that cod stocks have been depleted, other fish are used. In this recipe, we've replaced the fish with mussels and green tomato chow commonly served with fish cakes with apple chutney. If you haven't tried apple with seafood, give it a go; it is a wonderful complement.

■   ■

APPLE CHUTNEY

1   Core and dice the apples.

2   In a frying pan, melt the butter over medium heat and add the apple pieces. Bring to a boil, and stir in the brown sugar and cinnamon. Reduce the heat and simmer until the apples are tender, stirring occasionally. Can be served hot or cold.

MUSSEL POTATO CAKES

3   Rinse the mussels under running fresh water. Throw away any that do not close.

4   In a large pot, add the apple juice and mussels. Cover with a lid and cook on high for approximately 5 to 6 minutes or until steam is pouring out from under the lid.

5   Let the mussels cool. Remove the mussel meat from the shells and put it in a covered bowl or dish. Reserve half a cup (125 mL) of the broth.

6   Place the onions and mussel broth in a sauté pan and bring
    to a boil. Reduce the heat to a simmer and cook until the
    onions are soft and the liquid is reduced by half.

7   Place the mashed potatoes, onions, broth, parsley, summer
    savory, eggs and mussel meat in a large bowl. Gently mix
    by hand. Form into 3-ounce (100 g) cakes and coat lightly
    with flour.

8   Fry the mussel cakes in butter over medium heat until
    crisp and golden brown on both sides.

MUSSEL AND TOMATO RIGATONI

{Serves 4}

2 Tbsp (30 mL) olive oil

2 cloves garlic, chopped

½ cup (125 mL) diced leeks, white parts only

20 sweet basil leaves

1 tsp (5 mL) dried oregano

two 28 oz (796 mL) cans whole tomatoes

2 Tbsp (30 mL) tomato paste

1 cup (250 mL) red wine

1 lb (500 g) mussels

2 cups (500 mL) rigatoni pasta, cooked as per the instructions on the package, al dente

⅛ cup (30 mL) grated Parmesan cheese

THERE IS NOTHING more comforting than a big bowl of pasta. For the wine in this sauce, choose a wine that you would like to drink, and then serve the rest of the bottle with dinner.

1   Rinse the mussels under running fresh water. Throw away any that do not close.

2   In a large sauté pan, heat the olive oil over medium-high heat. Add the garlic, leeks, basil and oregano, and sauté until the garlic is soft. Add the tomatoes and with the back of a spoon, break them up, add the tomato paste and red wine. Reduce the heat and simmer for 20 minutes.

3   Add the mussels and cover to allow the mussels to cook slowly in the sauce. Once the mussels are open, remove them from the pot. Reduce the heat to low and cook until the sauce reduces by half (about 20 minutes).

4   Place the pasta in the bottom of your serving bowls. Top with the sauce and add the mussels and a sprinkling of grated Parmesan.

5   Serve with crusty garlic bread and the rest of your favourite red wine.

MUSSELS CARBONARA

{Serves 4}

MUSSELS

2 lb (1 kg) fresh mussels

½ cup (125 mL) white wine

PASTA

1 lb (500 g) package spaghetti
  (or linguini)

8 cups (2 litres) water

2 Tbsp (30mL) salt

SAUCE

1 Tbsp (15 mL) olive oil

2 cloves garlic, sliced

½ cup (125 mL) small cubes
  of pancetta

½ cup (125 mL) finely grated
  Parmesan cheese

2 eggs

½ tsp (2.5 mL) salt

½ cup (125 mL) cream (35%)

salt and pepper to taste

2 Tbsp (30 mL) finely chopped
  chives

THIS IS A twist on the classic dish, which has many variations but always uses pasta, eggs, cheese and bacon. There is a debate about whether you should add cream. Linda prefers to use it, as she thinks it gives the sauce a better texture. It's your choice.

■   ■

MUSSELS

1   Rinse the mussels under running fresh water. Throw away any that do not close.

2   In a large pot, add the mussels and wine. Cover with a lid and cook on high for approximately 5 to 6 minutes or until steam is pouring out from under the lid.

3   Let the mussels cool. Remove the mussel meat from the shells and put it in a covered bowl or dish to keep warm.

PASTA

4   In a large saucepan add water and salt. Bring the water to rolling boil and add the spaghetti. Cook until al a dente according to the instructions on the package. Drain and cover.

SAUCE

5   In a pan, add the olive oil, garlic and pancetta, and cook about 4 to 5 minutes, until the pancetta is crispy. Drain onto a paper towel.

6   In a bowl, whisk together the cheese, eggs, salt and cream and set aside.

7   Working quickly, add the egg mixture to the hot pasta, stirring to let the eggs cook through and the cheese melt.

8   Add the mussels and pancetta, season with salt and pepper and toss to combine.

9   Using tongs, place into a large bowl, sprinkle with the chives and serve immediately. .

SEAFOOD NAPOLEON

{Serves 2}

2 lb (1 kg) mussels

6 large scallops

12 shrimp (20–25 size)

⅓ cup (80 mL) Rosemary Dijon
   Butter (page 181)

½ cup (125 mL) *brunoise*
   mushrooms

½ cup (125 mL) *brunoise* red
   onions

¼ cup (60 mL) *brunoise* celery

2 bay leaves

½ cup (125mL) white wine

1 oz (30 mL) cognac

salt

ground pepper

½ cup (125 mL) cream (35%)

2 sheets 4- × 4-inch (10 × 10 cm)
   puff pastry, baked

½ lemon cut in wedges

3 sprigs of chopped chives

THIS DISH IS a Bossé family favourite. The flaky puff pastry is the perfect vehicle for the rich and decadent sauce. Don't be alarmed by the term *brunoise*. It simply means to dice by first cutting the vegetables in a julienne, then turning a quarter turn and cutting again. You should have a fine dice of ⅛ inch (3 mm) or less when you are finished.

1   Rinse the mussels under running fresh water. Throw away any that do not close.

2   Use a paper towel to dry off the scallops and shrimp. Remove the orange parts of the scallops and discard.

3   Melt two-thirds of the Rosemary Dijon Butter over high heat and sear the scallops and shrimp for 2 minutes on each side, remove to a separate plate.

4   Add the rest of the butter to the pan and sauté the mushrooms, onions and celery. Put in the bay leaves and deglaze the pan with the white wine and cognac.

5   Add the mussels and cover. Cook the mussels for 5 to 6 minutes or until steam is pouring out from under the lid. Remove the mussels and set aside.

6   Reduce the heat. Add the salt, pepper and cream and allow to reduce and thicken. Stir occasionally.

7   Remove the meat from the mussels and add them back into the sauce along with the scallops and shrimp.

8   Separate the puff pastry into 4 layers. Place the shrimp on the first layer, mussels on the second layer and scallops on the third layer and top with the fourth piece of puff pastry. Ladle the remaining sauce overtop. Garnish with the lemon wedges and chives.

MUSSEL STRUDEL

{Serves 6}

SALSA

1 tsp (5 mL) vegetable oil

1 Tbsp (15 mL) honey

juice of half a lime

1 mango, peeled and diced

1 cup (250 mL) diced peaches,
  fresh or frozen

½ cup (125 mL) diced red onion

1 red chili, deveined with seeds
  removed, finely diced

½ tsp (2.5 mL) salt

MUSSELS

2 lb (1 kg) mussels

½ cup (125 mL) white wine

STRUDEL

2 Tbsp (30 mL) butter

½ medium white onion, chopped

2 cloves garlic, chopped

2 Tbsp (30 mL) drained capers

2 tsp (10 mL) fresh thyme

½ cup (125 mL) cream cheese

¼ cup (60 mL) Parmesan cheese

½ cup (125 mL) black olives,
  pitted and cut in half

Linda loves making strudels for fruit and chicken—why not a mussel strudel? You can make this recipe ahead, store it in the refrigerator and then pop it in the oven when you are ready. This recipe is rich, but you can serve small slices and set it off with a salad of greens and herbs. The secret is to have good-quality puff pastry and a tasty salsa to accompany it.

SALSA

1   In a bowl mix the vegetable oil, honey, lime juice and salt, then add the mango, peach, onions and red chili and, with a spoon, stir so that the fruit is well covered. Place in a covered dish and put in the refrigerator to allow the flavours to meld for about an hour.

MUSSELS

2   Rinse the mussels under running fresh water. Throw away any that do not close.

3   In a large pot, add the mussels and half the wine. Cover with a lid and cook on high for approximately 5 to 6 minutes or until steam is pouring out from under the lid.

4   Once the mussels are cool, remove the meat from the shells and refrigerate.

STRUDEL

5   Preheat oven to 375°F (190°C).

6   Heat up a large frying pan, add the butter followed by the onion, garlic and capers. Sauté until the onions are brown stirring frequently.

½ cup (125 mL) cream (35%)

1 cup (250 mL) fresh whole
   wheat breadcrumbs

zest of half a lemon

frozen puff pastry, thawed and
   rolled out to a 9 × 12-inch
   (23 × 30 cm) sheet

1 egg, beaten

7   Add the rest of the wine to deglaze the pan and capture all
    the flavours. Add the thyme, cream cheese and Parmesan
    cheese and heat until the cheese has melted. Stir in the
    mussels, olives, cream and breadcrumbs. Remove from the
    heat and set aside.

8   Put some parchment paper on a baking sheet and lay out
    the puff pastry. Spoon the mussel mixture onto the pastry,
    fold over and fold the ends. Turn the strudel over and make
    4 cuts in the top to let the steam out. Brush with the egg.

9   Bake for 30 to 40 minutes until golden brown.

10 When you take the strudel out of the oven, give it about
    5 minutes to cool. Use a serrated knife to cut the strudel,
    and serve with the salsa on the side.

ASPARAGUS

with Mussel and Gorgonzola Sauce

{Serves 4}

2 lb (1 kg) mussels

¼ cup (60 mL) white wine

¼ cup (60 mL) water

1 bunch asparagus

1 Tbsp (15 mL) butter

¼ cup (60 mL) cream (35%)

3 oz (85 g) Gorgonzola cheese,
　　cut in pieces

2 Tbsp (30 mL) pomegranate
　　seeds, for garnish

THIS IS A wonderful recipe in the spring, when asparagus is at its best. It uses some of Linda's favourite ingredients—gorgonzola and asparagus—looks amazing on the plate and best of all, it only takes 15 minutes to make a great dish. The sauce is creamy and salty to balance the asparagus. Linda has eaten asparagus all her life. As a small child she used to help her grandmother pull the tender shoots from a patch in her flower garden—not the vegetable garden because she loved the feathery bush too. You may end up with more sauce than you need; you can reheat and serve it on toast the next day.

■ ■

1　Rinse the mussels under running fresh water. Throw away any that do not close.

2　In a large pot, add the mussels and wine. Cover with a lid and cook on high for approximately 5 to 6 minutes or until steam is pouring out from under the lid.

3　Once the mussels are cool, remove the meat from the shells and set aside. Reserve ¼ cup (60 mL) of the broth.

4　In a wide mouth saucepan or frying pan, bring the water to a boil. Snap the bottom ends off the asparagus and drop the whole stalks into the boiling water.

5　In a second saucepan, melt the butter. Slowly add the cream and the reserved mussel broth and cook for 5 minutes on medium heat. Add the Gorgonzola cheese and whisk until the cheese has melted. Cook for another 3 to 4 minutes. Keep the mixture bubbly but not roaring, and stir constantly.

6　Add the mussels to the sauce and stir for another minute.

7　Drain the asparagus and divide among 4 plates. Spoon the sauce over the asparagus, leaving the tips uncovered. Spoon equal amounts of the mussels over the asparagus, sprinkle with the pomegranate seeds and serve.

FLORENTINE MUSSEL BENEDICT

{Serves 4}

MUSSEL BENEDICT

2 lb (1 kg) mussels

¼ cup (60 mL) white wine

1 tsp (5 mL) white vinegar

4 large eggs

1 Tbsp (15 mL) olive oil

1 cup (250 mL) baby spinach

4 crumpets

½ tsp (2.5 mL) salt

E GGS BENEDICT IS most often served at brunch, but paired with a side salad, it will make a very elegant lunch or a light dinner. Don't be intimidated by the homemade hollandaise. It's not as complicated as everyone thinks, and once you've had the real thing, you won't want to go back to pre-packaged sauce.

■ ──────────── ■

MUSSEL BENEDICT

1 Rinse the mussels under running fresh water. Throw away any that do not close.

2 In a large pot, add the mussels and wine. Cover with a lid and cook on high for approximately 5 to 6 minutes or until steam is pouring out from under the lid.

3 Let the mussels cool. Remove the mussel meat from the shells and put it in a covered bowl or dish to keep warm.

4 Place two to three inches of water in a non-stick pan, add the vinegar and bring to a simmer over medium-high heat. Crack the first egg into a small bowl and gently slide it into the water. Repeat with the other eggs and cook to the desired consistency. Using a slotted spoon, remove to a plate and set aside.

5 Drain the water from the pan, return to medium heat and add the olive oil and the spinach. Sauté until the spinach has wilted.

6 While this is happening, toast the crumpets. When the spinach has wilted, sprinkle it with the salt.

HOLLANDAISE

4 egg yolks

1 Tbsp (15 mL) cold water

1¼ cups (310 mL) butter

1½ tsp (7.5 mL) lemon juice

pinch of cayenne

HOLLANDAISE

7 Place a double boiler over medium heat. Once the water has reached a simmer, add the egg yolks and water, and whisk to mix. Gradually whisk in the butter and finish with the lemon juice and cayenne pepper, continuing to whisk until the sauce thickens. Keep the sauce warm until you are ready to serve it.

ASSEMBLY

8 Divide the spinach evenly between the 4 crumpets. Add the poached egg, place the mussel meat around the egg and cover with hollandaise sauce.

⚓
ROOT BEER MUSSELS
{Serves 2}

2 lb (1 kg) mussels
½ cup (125 mL) root beer
¼ cup (60 mL) minced shallots

THIS FUN RECIPE is very simple and will definitely bring out the child in you. It might be a neat way to get the kids to try a new food.

■   ■

1   Rinse the mussels under running fresh water. Throw away any that do not close.

2   In a large pot, add the mussels, root beer and shallots. Cover with a lid and cook on high for approximately 5 to 6 minutes or until steam is pouring out from under the lid.

3   Spoon the mussels in a large bowl to serve family-style and pour the broth overtop.

4   Serve with crusty bread and potato chips.

PINEAPPLE SZECHUAN MUSSEL PIZZA

{Serves 4}

MUSSELS

3 lb (1.8 kg) mussels

½ cup (125 mL) white wine

SAUCE

¼ cup (60 mL) dried Szechuan
  peppers

1 cup (250 mL) pure maple syrup

INGREDIENTS CONTINUE...

THIS PIZZA DEVELOPED out of another of Alain's recipes. He originally made the Szechuan sauce as an accompaniment for beef tenderloin. The next evening, he was doing a "clean out the refrigerator" dinner, and a bit of the leftover sauce evolved into this pizza. It has become a family favourite.

◼   ◼

MUSSELS

1 Rinse the mussels under running fresh water. Throw away any that do not close.

2 In a large pot, add the mussels and wine. Cover with a lid and cook on high for approximately 5 to 6 minutes or until steam is pouring out from under the lid.

3 Once the mussels are cool, remove the meat from the shells, put in a covered dish and refrigerate.

SAUCE

4 In a saucepan, toast the Szechuan peppers over medium heat for 2 to 3 minutes until fragrant. Add the maple syrup, bring to a boil then remove from heat and let sit until cool.

5 Strain the sauce using a fine mesh strainer or cheesecloth. Discard the peppers and reserve the sauce.

METHOD CONTINUES...

PINEAPPLE SZECHUAN MUSSEL PIZZA

{CONTINUED}

PIZZA

4 pieces naan bread

2 Tbsp (30 mL) olive oil

1 cup (250 mL) fresh pineapple
chunks

1 tsp (5 mL) coarse salt

4 sprigs cilantro, torn

¼ cup (60 mL) shaved Parmesan
cheese

2 Tbsp (30 mL) crumbled blue
cheese

PIZZA

1 Preheat the oven to 450°F (230°C).

2 Brush the naan bread with the olive oil. Divide the mussel
meat evenly between the four pieces of bread. Do the same
with the pineapple chunks, and sprinkle with the salt
and cilantro. Drizzle with a quarter cup (60 mL) of the
Szechuan maple sauce, top with Parmesan shavings and
crumble small pieces of blue cheese on top.

3 Place pizzas on a large baking sheet, and bake until the
cheese melts and begins to brown, approximately 8 to 10
minutes.

SWEET CHILI PIZZA

{Serves 2}

MUSSELS

1 lb (500 g) mussels

¼ cup (60 mL) white wine

¼ cup (60 mL) sweet chili sauce

VEGETABLES

4 asparagus spears

½ cup (125 mL) red onion, sliced

1 yellow pepper, julienne

2 portobello mushrooms, sliced

2 Tbsp (30 mL) olive oil

½ tsp (2.5 mL) ground pepper

FLATBREAD PIZZAS ARE all the rage these days—and for good reason: they are fast and tasty. Don't be discouraged by all the steps in this recipe. They can easily be broken down and completed ahead of time so that the only thing left to do at mealtime is put the pizza together.

■   ■

MUSSELS

1   Rinse the mussels under running fresh water. Throw away any that do not close.

2   Place the mussels in a medium-sized pot. Add the white wine and sweet chili sauce, cover and place over high heat. Cook for 4 to 5 minutes or until steam is pouring out from under the lid. Shake a few times to coat the mussels with the chili sauce.

3   Let the mussels cool. Remove the mussel meat from the shells and put it in a covered bowl or dish to keep warm.

4   On medium heat, reduce the broth until it turns into a thick sauce (approximately 10–15 minutes).

VEGETABLES

5   In a bowl, toss the asparagus, onion, yellow pepper, and mushrooms with the olive oil and pepper.

6   Put the vegetables on a flat grill or barbecue and grill until the edges starts to char, about 4 to 5 minutes. Let rest.

REDUCTION

1 cup (250 mL) balsamic vinegar

PIZZA

2 pieces flatbread

1 Tbsp (15 mL) olive oil

6 oz (175 g) bocconcini cheese, sliced

1 cup (250 mL) arugula

REDUCTION

7 Place the balsamic vinegar in a small pot and bring to a boil. Turn the heat to low and reduce until it is thick enough to coat the back of a spoon.

PIZZA

8 Brush the flatbread with olive oil and top with the grilled vegetables, thickened mussel broth, mussel meat and bocconcini. Place under the broiler for 3 to 4 minutes to warm up.

9 Finish with a handful of arugula drizzled with the balsamic vinegar reduction.

Caramelized Onion and
GOAT CHEESE PIZZA
{Serves 2}

MUSSELS

2 lb (1 kg) mussels

1½ cups (375 mL) port

ONIONS

¼ lb (125 g) butter

4 medium sweet onions, julienne

½ cup (125 mL) maple syrup

¼ tsp (1 mL) salt

½ tsp (2.5 mL) pepper

Т**HIS PIZZA HAS** wonderful earthy colours. The port gives the caramelized onions an amazing rich flavour. The onion recipe is a versatile dish to have in your repertoire. They are delicious served on crostini with goat cheese as an appetizer or underneath a bed of grilled scallops as an entrée.

■   ■

MUSSELS

1   Rinse the mussels under running fresh water. Throw away any that do not close.

2   In a medium-sized pot, add the mussels and a half cup (125 mL) of the port. Cover with a lid and cook on high for approximately 5 to 6 minutes or until steam is pouring out from under the lid.

3   Let the mussels cool. Remove the mussel meat from the shells and put it in a covered bowl or dish. Reserve the broth.

ONIONS

4   Melt the butter in a large frying pan. When it just begins to brown, add the onions and cook until translucent. Add the maple syrup, a half cup of the reserved mussel broth, the rest of the port, salt and pepper. Bring to a boil, reduce until as little liquid as possible remains without the having the onions stick to the pan.

PIZZA

2 medium-sized flatbreads

2 Tbsp (30 mL) olive oil

½ tsp (2.5 mL) coarse salt

½ cup (125 mL) crumbled goat
cheese

PIZZA

5   Preheat oven to 350°F (175°C).

6   Brush the flatbreads with the olive oil, and sprinkle with
the coarse salt. Warm in a frying pan on each side over
medium heat for 1 to 2 minutes until soft. Add 4 Tbsp
(60 mL) of the caramelized onions, the mussel meat and
the goat cheese.

7   Cook in the oven for 8 to 10 minutes.

PERNOD CREAM MUSSELS

{Serves 4}

5 lb (2.2 kg) mussels

1 tsp (5 mL) butter

1 tsp (5 mL) olive oil

1 small onion, diced

1 garlic clove

½ cup (125 mL) finely chopped fennel

½ cup (125 mL) white wine

1½ oz (45 mL) Pernod

½ cup (125 mL) cream (35%)

2 Tbsp (30 mL) finely chopped parsley or chives

DO YOU LIKE the taste of liquorice, fennel or anise? With this recipe, you have hints of all these beautiful flavours combined with a creamy, sweet sauce on your mussels. Your guests will be asking for more, so cook lots.

1   Rinse the mussels under running fresh water. Throw away any that do not close.

2   In a saucepan, melt the butter with the oil. Add the onion, garlic and fennel and cook, stirring for 6 to 8 minutes.

3   Add the mussels and wine and cover with a lid. Cook on high heat for 6 to 8 minutes or until steam starts to pour out from under the lid.

4   Using a slotted spoon, divide the mussels into the four bowls and cover with foil. Add the Pernod to the broth, stir thoroughly and then add the cream. Let the mixture simmer for 5 minutes,

5   Pour the broth over the mussels. Sprinkle the fresh parsley or chives overtop and serve.

⚓

MUSSEL COULIBIAC
with Roasted Red Pepper Sauce
{Serves 4}

COULIBIAC, ORIGINALLY FROM Russia, is traditionally made with salmon, hard-boiled eggs and rice wrapped in pastry. Eventually the French adopted this dish, and it grew in popularity. Today, many versions are served around the world. If you can't find glass noodles, use rice instead. The sweet basil pesto recipe included makes more than this recipe requires. It will store well in the refrigerator for at least a week. It can be spread on bread for sandwiches or makes a great sauce for pasta.

■   ■

VEGETABLES
3 Tbsp (45 mL) olive oil

1 Tbsp (15 mL) red wine vinegar

1 tsp (5 mL) salt

2 cups (500 mL) chopped vegetables, such as mushrooms, asparagus, red onions or red peppers

PESTO
½ cup (125 mL) fresh basil

½ cup (125 mL) pine nuts

juice of 1 lime

½ cup (125 mL) Parmesan cheese

½ cup (125 mL) olive oil

salt to taste

MUSSELS
2 lb (1 kg) mussels

¼ cup (60 mL) white wine

INGREDIENTS CONTINUE...

VEGETABLES

1 In a bowl, mix the olive oil, vinegar and salt. Add the vegetables and toss to coat them.

2 On a baking sheet, spread out the vegetables and roast in a 400°F (200°C) oven for 20 to 25 minutes.

PESTO

3 Place the basil, pine nuts, lime juice and Parmesan in the bowl of a food processor. Pulse until it reaches the desired consistency of a coarse paste. Add the olive oil in a slow, steady stream while the processor is running. Add salt to taste.

MUSSELS

4 Rinse the mussels under running fresh water. Throw away any that do not close.

5 In a large pot, add the mussels and wine. Cover with a lid and cook on high for approximately 5 to 6 minutes or until steam is pouring out from under the lid.

METHOD CONTINUES...

MUSSEL COULIBIAC
WITH ROASTED RED PEPPER SAUCE
{CONTINUED}

ROASTED RED PEPPER SAUCE

one 19 oz (540 mL) jar roasted
   red peppers, drained
½ cup (125 mL) olive oil
½ cup (125 mL) mussel broth
2 tsp (10 mL) red wine vinegar

ASSEMBLY

two 9- × 12-inch (23 × 30 cm)
   sheets puff pastry
½ cup (125 mL) sweet basil pesto
1 cup (250 mL) baby spinach
1 bag glass noodles cooked
   according to package
   instructions
roasted vegetables
mussel meat
¼ cup (60 mL) red pepper sauce
2 eggs and 1 Tbsp (15 mL) water,
   mixed together (egg wash)

6   Let the mussels cool. Remove the mussel meat from the shells and put it in a covered bowl or dish. Reserve the broth.

ROASTED RED PEPPER SAUCE

7   Place the roasted red peppers and olive oil in a food processor and purée. Add the mussel broth and vinegar and process until smooth.

ASSEMBLY

8   Preheat the oven to 350°F (175°C).

9   Place one sheet of puff pastry on a greased baking sheet. Ladle a half cup (125 mL) of pesto down the centre and cover with the spinach. Add the glass noodles, roasted vegetables and cooked mussel meat. Add a quarter cup (60 mL) of red pepper sauce.

10   Brush the edge of the puff pastry with the egg wash and place the other sheet of puff pastry on top. Press down on the edge to seal, and cut 4 vents on the top pastry layer to let the steam escape. Brush the top of the pastry with the egg wash, and bake for 20 to 25 minutes.

11   Remove from the oven, cut into portions and serve with the roasted red pepper sauce on top.

MUSSEL RISOTTO

CHEF MARINO D'ANTONIO, OPERA BOMBANA, BEIJING, CHINA

{Serves 6}

5 lb (2.2 kg) mussels

1¼ cups (310 mL) white wine

¾ cup (185 mL) minced shallots

6 Tbsp (90mL) olive oil

¼ cup (60 mL) butter

1½ cups (375 mL) Aquarello rice
(or another short-grain rice)

2 Tbsp (30 mL) chopped pitted
black olives

1½ Tbsp (22.5 mL) chopped
capers

1 garlic clove, chopped

2 sprigs fresh thyme

2 Tbsp (30 mL) mascarpone

zest of half an orange, minced

3½ Tbsp (55 mL) Parmigiano
Reggiano

3 leaves of marjoram

CHEF MARINO AND ALAIN have worked together at the World Culinary Summit, the Right Some Good festival in Cape Breton and numerous other events since then. It was Marino who taught Alain the proper way to make a risotto, so Alain felt it would be fitting to have Marino contribute one of his famous risottos to this cookbook.

■ ■

1   Rinse the mussels under running fresh water. Throw away any that do not close.

2   In a large pot, add the mussels and a half cup (125 mL) of the wine. Cover with a lid and cook on high for approximately 6 to 8 minutes or until steam is pouring out from under the lid.

3   Let the mussels cool. Remove the mussel meat from the shells and put it in a covered bowl or dish. Reserve 4 cups (1 L) of the broth.

4   In a large pot, cook the shallots with 2 Tbsp (30 mL) of the olive oil and 1 Tbsp (15mL) of the butter. When they are translucent, add the rice. Once it begins to stick to the pan, add ¾ of a cup (185 mL) of the white wine. Take off the heat and set aside.

5   In another pot, put the olives, capers and a half cup (125 mL) of mussel broth, then add the rice. Cook at a low temperature. Once the liquid has been absorbed, add another half cup (125 mL) of broth. Stir, and repeat the process until all of the mussel broth has been incorporated into the rice.

6   Sauté the mussel meat for 1 minute in a pan with 2 Tbsp (30 mL) olive oil, garlic and thyme and set aside.

7   Once the rice is almost ready (softened), add the remaining butter, the remaining olive oil and the mascarpone, and mix. Add the mussels and the orange zest, mix, and finish with the Parmigiano Reggiano and marjoram.

MUSSEL FISH PIE
{Serves 6}

This recipe is a variation of the popular English fish pie. The first time Linda had fish pie, she was surprised and delighted at the flavour this dish had with very simple ingredients. In this recipe, she has taken advantage of the attributes of the mussel broth, which intensifies the flavour of the dish. This version is inspired by her absolutely favourite English chef, Delia Smith, whose recipes are a regular part of her repertoire of dishes. As a variation, you may wish to add savoury pie crust on the bottom of this dish.

SEAFOOD

2 lb (1 kg) mussels, cooked and shucked as described in Simple Steamed Mussels (page 96)

1 cup (250 mL) mussel broth from Simple Steamed Mussels (page 96)

5 Tbsp (75 mL) butter

½ cup (125 mL) finely diced onion

1 bay leaf

1½ lb (750 g) firm white fish, cut into 4-inch (10 cm) pieces

SAUCE

2 Tbsp (30 mL) flour

½ cup (125 mL) cream (35%)

2 Tbsp (30 mL) chopped dill

salt and pepper to taste

SEAFOOD

1   In a saucepan over medium heat, melt 1 Tbsp (15 mL) of the butter and sauté the onions. Add the mussel broth, bay leaf and fish to the pan and poach for about 5 minutes. Remove the fish and set to drain, but keep the broth. The fish will be slightly underdone.

SAUCE

2   In a separate pan, melt 2 Tbsp (30 mL) of the butter. Add the flour and whisk together. Slowly add the broth left from cooking the fish, and let the sauce cook on medium heat for about 5 minutes. Add the cream, dill, and salt and pepper and take off the stove.

3   Place the fish in a deep pie dish and cover with the mussels and sauce. Sir gently to coat the ingredients.

TOPPING

6 large white potatoes

½ bulb celery root

¼ cup (60 mL) cream (35%)

TOPPING

4   Preheat the oven to 375°F (190°C).

5   In a medium pan, boil the potatoes and celery root together until soft. Drain and mash, adding the rest of the butter and the cream.

6   Place spoonfuls of the mash on top of the mussels and fish and smooth them until you have the whole dish covered.

7   Bake for about 45 to 50 minutes or until the potato topping is golden and the pie is bubbling. You may want to put a baking sheet under the pie dish in case the pie bubbles over.

8   Let rest for 5 minutes before serving with some cooked green vegetables or a peppery leaf salad.

CAPE ISLANDER SALMON

{Serves 2}

SAUCE

1 Tbsp (15 mL) butter

½ cup (125 mL) diced shallots

¼ cup (60 mL) fresh dill

½ cup (125 mL) prepared yellow
    mustard

1 cup (250 mL) maple syrup

SALMON

12 to 14 cooked mussels, meat
    only, prepared as described in
    Simple Steamed Mussels
    (page 96)

4 sprigs chives, chopped

1 Tbsp (15 mL) dry breadcrumbs

½ tsp (2.5 mL) Old Bay
    Seasoning

1 tsp (5 mL) grated Parmesan
    cheese

two 6 oz (175 g) salmon fillets

THIS IS ONE of the dishes of Alain's that gets requested time and time again. The maple mustard sauce is what makes it so special. The secret is the plain yellow mustard. If you try to "fancy it up" with any other type of mustard, it just won't work.

SAUCE

1 Melt the butter in a small saucepan. Sauté the shallots and dill until soft, and then add the mustard and maple and bring to a boil. Reduce the heat and simmer for 10 minutes.

SALMON

2 Preheat your oven to 400°F (200°C)

3 Combine the mussels, chives, breadcrumbs, Old Bay Seasoning and Parmesan cheese.

4 Make a horizontal slit on the side of the salmon fillet and stuff with the mussel mixture.

5 Place the salmon on a baking sheet lined with parchment paper, and bake for 20 to 22 minutes.

6 To serve the salmon, ladle the dill sauce on top or serve on the side.

HALIBUT WITH MUSSEL CREAM

{Serves 2}

1 lb (500 g) mussels

2 Tbsp (30 mL) flour

two 6 oz (175 g) halibut fillets

salt and pepper to taste

1 Tbsp (15 mL) butter

1 tsp (5 mL) Dijon mustard

2 sprigs rosemary

½ cup (125 mL) white wine

½ cup (125 mL) cream (35%)

HALIBUT IS A wonderful firm-fleshed fish that holds up exceptionally well to pan frying. Because it has a stronger flavour than other white fish, the rich cream sauce really balances it nicely. This is a dish that can easily be doubled, since it is special enough to serve to guests.

1 Rinse the mussels under running fresh water. Throw away any that do not close.

2 Preheat the oven to 200°F (95°C).

3 Lightly flour the halibut fillets and season with salt and pepper.

4 Melt the butter in a frying pan over medium-high heat. Add the halibut and cook evenly on for 3 minutes on each side. Place the fish on a baking sheet lined with parchment paper and let rest in the preheated oven.

5 Add the mustard and rosemary to the frying pan. Simmer for one minute, and then deglaze the pan with the wine, increase the heat to high, add the mussels and cover.

6 Cook for 4 to 5 minutes or until the mussels open. With a slotted spoon, remove the mussel meat and set aside. Bring the broth to a boil and reduce by half. Add the cream and allow the sauce to reduce until it coats the back of a spoon.

7 Place the halibut fillets onto two plates. Divide the mussels and spoon on top of the halibut. Pour the sauce over the top and serve.

Chapter 5

ON
THE GRILL
'N' IN
THE OVEN

GRILLING TIPS

GRILLING MUSSELS

You can cook mussels on the grill. Just be sure to watch them carefully so they don't burn. Keep a spray bottle close at hand and mist the mussels from time to time. Try putting a little white wine or beer in the spray bottle so you are adding extra flavour at the same time!

GRILLING BREAD

Alain recommends that you cut your crusty bread thicker than you would at the table. Spread it with butter, such as our Rosemary Dijon Butter (page 181) or Honey Basil Butter (page 184) on both sides, and wait until your guests are ready to sit at the table before grilling the bread. He finds it does not take long and it is always a big hit when delivered to your guests piping hot. Grill it on medium heat and flip it often to avoid burning.

GRILLING VEGETABLES

These are two ways Alain likes to grill vegetables. The first is to simply cut the vegetables into big pieces and brush them with olive oil and salt. Use eggplant, zucchini cut lengthwise, large slices of red onions, chunks of pepper, squash, etc. Cutting them into ¼-inch-thick (6 mm) pieces gives them

a chance to capture the flavour from the grill.

The second way is to marinate your vegetables and cook them in a grilling basket. It brings out the natural sugars and is tasty but does not necessarily give the charred flavour the grill is so famous for.

Lastly if you feel up to having fun, put them directly on the grill. You will need to watch them so they don't fall in between the cracks. I love doing asparagus, mushrooms, onions, whole tomatoes, etc. With a simple marinade of olive oil, salt, pepper and balsamic vinegar, this never misses.

Who doesn't look forward to the arrival of garden-grown corn with unabated anticipation? Usually Alain eats them in the traditional way, which is boiling them and smothering with butter, but occasionally he cooks them on the grill. Simply pull back the husk, remove the tassels (silky strands) and bring the husk back around the ear. Soak the corn in cold water for a few minutes, and grill it over medium heat, rotating frequently. Another method if you like a more charred flavour is to simply peel the corn and place it on an oiled, heated grill. Use tongs to turn it very frequently so it doesn't burn.

HOT GRILLED MUSSELS

with Pineapple Mango Salsa

{Serves 2}

SALSA

4 Tbsp (60 mL) lime juice

4 Tbsp (60 mL) chopped cilantro
(you can also use mint)

½ tsp (2.5 mL) salt

pinch of chili pepper flakes

2 Tbsp (30 mL) olive oil

2 cups (500 mL) finely diced
pineapple

2 cups (500 mL) finely diced
mango

1 cup (250 mL) finely diced red
onion

1 cup (250 mL) diced English
cucumber

MUSSELS

2 lb (1 kg) mussels

1 cup (250 mL) light beer, in a
spray bottle

THE PINEAPPLE MANGO salsa recipe makes a generous amount. It is wonderful with the mussels, and you can enjoy the leftovers with nacho chips. You can also put some foil on the top of the grill, crimping the edges, and place the mussels on top instead of directly on the grill surface.

■　　　　　　　　■

SALSA

1　In a medium bowl, add the lime juice, cilantro, salt, chili flakes and olive oil and whisk until well mixed.

2　Add the pineapple, mango, onion and cucumber and toss to make sure they are covered by the sauce. Cover and put in the refrigerator to chill for approximately one hour.

MUSSELS

3　Rinse the mussels under running fresh water. Throw away any that do not close.

4　Turn your barbecue on and bring to a medium temperature.

5　Using tongs, place the mussels on the grill. Spray the mussels with beer.

6　Continuously spray the beer over the mussels to keep them from burning. After 4 or 5 minutes, they will start to open.

7　Remove the opened mussels from the barbecue and place them on a platter.

8　Serve with the salsa on the side.

COTTAGE-STYLE GRILLED MUSSELS

{Serves 1}

1 lb (500 g) mussels

1 garlic clove, chopped

½ tsp (2.5 mL) fresh ginger, peeled and minced

half a lime

2 oz (60 mL) of your favourite beverage

THIS RECIPE IS a throwback to Alain's Boy Scout days. That is where he first learned to cook. This is a recipe that gets everyone involved! It can be done on a barbecue or over a campfire or fire pit. Multiply the ingredients for this recipe by the number of people you have in your party.

◼ ◼

1   Rinse the mussels under running fresh water. Throw away any that do not close.

2   Provide each guest with a 12- × 12-inch (30 × 30 cm) piece of thick foil.

3   Place 1 lb (500 g) of fresh mussel in the centre, add crushed garlic, minced ginger and a squeeze of lime. Shape the foil around the mussels to make a bowl and add your favourite beverage, be it wine, beer or a non-alcoholic drink such as apple juice or root beer for the kids. Close the top to form a "purse," leaving a small opening for the steam to vent.

4   Place the packets on the barbecue or coals and let them steam away. After 5 to 6 minutes, carefully remove the foil packet from the fire and allow to cool. Open and enjoy.

BARBECUE BEER MUSSELS

{Serves 6}

5 lb (2.2 kg) mussels

8 slices bacon, cut into 1-inch (2.5 cm) squares

1 small onion, finely chopped

¼ cup (60 mL) finely chopped fennel

¼ cup (60 mL) finely chopped carrots

1 garlic clove, sliced

1 bottle of your favourite beer— half for the dish and half for the cook to drink

2 Tbsp (30 mL) barbecue sauce

1 Tbsp (15 mL) chopped fresh parsley

½ cup (125 mL) melted butter

THIS IS A great recipe to make on the side burner of your barbecue while you focus on the meat on the main grill. Linda's family usually dips steamed mussels in melted butter regardless of what they have been steamed with, and this recipe is no different. This is a carryover from the same treatment with soft-shell clams.

1   Rinse the mussels under running fresh water. Throw away any that do not close.

2   In a large pot, add the bacon and stir until it is browned. Add the onion, fennel, carrots and garlic and stir for a couple of minutes. Add the mussels, pour in the beer and sprinkle the barbecue sauce overtop. Cover with a lid, and turn the heat up to the highest setting.

3   When steam starts to barrel out from under the lid, the mussels are ready (about 6 to 8 minutes).

4   Spoon into a big bowl for family-style eating, or into individual bowls, and sprinkle the fresh parsley on top.

5   Serve with crusty bread, and dip the mussels into melted butter before popping them in your mouth.

ASIAGO-STUFFED MUSSELS

{Serves 8}

2 lb (1 kg) mussels

¼ cup (60 mL) white wine

¼ cup (60 mL) finely chopped shallots

6 slices pancetta

½ cup (125 mL) butter

3 Tbsp (45 mL) chopped chives

1 cup (250 mL) panko crumbs

1 cup (250 mL) grated Asiago cheese

2 Tbsp (30 mL) chopped parsley

ORIGINALLY ASIAGO CHEESE came from the foothills of Italy's Veneto region. These days, cheese makers are producing Asiago here in North America, and it is readily available in our grocery stores. Cooks find it perfect for grating and a good alternative to Parmesan cheese. It pairs well with mussels, and this is a great party dish that you can make ahead and finish as your guests arrive.

1 Rinse the mussels under running fresh water. Throw away any that do not close.

2 In a large pot, add the mussels, wine and shallots. Cover with a lid and cook on high for approximately 5 to 6 minutes or until steam is pouring out from under the lid.

3 Let the mussels cool. Remove the mussel meat from the shells. Put it in a covered bowl or dish and refrigerate. Reserve the shells and break in half.

4 In a frying pan, add the pancetta and cook until crisp. Remove and crumble. In the same pan, add the butter, chives, panko and cheese (reserve 2 Tbsp/30 mL to use as garnish). Stir until the ingredients are mixed together and the butter and cheese have melted. Remove from the heat and add the pancetta, mixing thoroughly.

5 Lay out the half shells on a baking sheet. Place a mussel in each shell, and then use a teaspoon to top each mussel with some of the cheese mixture.

6 Bake in the oven at 375°F (190°C) for about 10 to 15 minutes, until they are golden and bubbly. Remove and put on a platter to serve. Sprinkle a little parsley and some of the remaining cheese on each shell to give it some colour.

MUSSEL MAC 'N' CHEESE

{Serves 6}

4 Tbsp (30 mL) butter
¾ cup (185 mL) panko crumbs
3 lb (1.8 kg) mussels
½ cup (125 mL) white wine
16 oz (625 g) bow tie pasta
2 Tbsp (30 mL) flour
1 cup (250 mL) whole milk
¼ cup (60 mL) fontina cheese
½ cup (125 mL) Gruyère cheese
1 Tbsp (15 mL) chopped chives
salt and white pepper to taste

WHO DOESN'T LIKE macaroni and cheese? Linda's daughter absolutely loved it growing up. She never knew what mac 'n' cheese was, having been raised outside of North America, and she loved cheese sauce. Linda has been experimenting with adding different ingredients to the cheese sauce and encourages you to be adventurous too. Lots of vegetables and proteins can be combined to make a more complex dish. This recipe starts with a cheese roux and a bowl of mussels, giving you a creamy, salty and tasty dish.

1   In a saucepan, melt 2 Tbsp (30 mL) of the butter and add the panko crumbs. Stir constantly until the panko crumbs are a golden brown, then remove from the heat and set aside.

2   Rinse the mussels under running fresh water. Throw away any that do not close.

3   In a large pot, add the mussels and wine. Cover with a lid and cook on high for approximately 6 to 7 minutes or until steam is pouring out from under the lid.

4   Once the mussels are cool, remove the meat from the shells.

5   Cook the pasta according to the instructions on the package until it is just al dente. Take off the heat, drain and pour back into the pot and cover to keep warm.

6   While the pasta is cooking, take a large shallow pan, melt the rest of the butter. When it is foaming, take off the burner.

METHOD CONTINUES...

7   Add the flour, and using a whisk, blend well. Slowly begin to add the milk, whisking continuously. Return to the burner and cook for 5 minutes. A good roux—which is what you are making here—is too often not cooked long enough, so you get the taste of flour. Season with salt and white pepper to taste.

8   Add the fontina and Gruyère cheeses, and cook for another 5 minutes until the cheese is melted and the flavours have come together.

ASSEMBLY

9   Add the pasta and mussels to the cheese sauce, stirring well to coat. Move the mixture to a greased casserole dish, cover with the buttered panko crumbs and put in a 350°F (175°C) oven for 15 to 20 minutes until well warmed through. Top with the chives and serve.

⚓
MUSSEL QUICHE
{Serves 6}

CRUST

½ cup (125 mL) cold butter,
   cut into cubes

1¼ cup (310 mL) all-purpose
   flour

2 egg yolks

pinch of salt

3 Tbsp (45 mL) ice water

INGREDIENTS CONTINUE...

Q UICHE MAKES A lovely light lunch. Serve it with a salad and a glass of wine, and it's the perfect meal. Divide the filling ingredients between mini tartlet shells, and you have wonderful hors d'oeuvres. The savoury short crust eliminates the usual sugar, using Parmesan cheese to give it a flavour that complements the richness rather than overwhelming it. The pie crust recipe is generous and you may end up with more than you need for this recipe. You can freeze any extra for future use.

◾━━━━━━━━━◾

CRUST

1   Preheat the oven to 350°F (175°C)

2   In a large glass bowl, rub the butter and the flour until granular. With your fingers, incorporate the egg yolks and salt. Knead together and add water as needed. Knead again on a floury surface, being careful not to overknead the dough.

3   Cover in plastic wrap and refrigerate for 15 minutes.

4   Roll out the dough on a floured surface. Place in a 9-inch (23 cm) deep pie plate and refrigerate for 10 minutes before putting in the oven for 20 minutes.

METHOD CONTINUES...

QUICHE

1 lb (500 g) mussels

¼ cup (60 mL) white wine

3 eggs, beaten

1 cup (250 mL) milk

1 cup (250 mL) cream (35%)

1 Tbsp (15 mL) mayonnaise

1 Tbsp (15 mL) butter

½ cup (125 mL) diced onions

¼ tsp (1 mL) tarragon

½ tsp (2.5 mL) salt

½ cup (125 mL) grated Gruyère
cheese

QUICHE

5   Rinse the mussels under running fresh water. Throw away any that do not close.

6   In a large pot, add the mussels and wine. Cover with a lid and cook on high for approximately 4 to 5 minutes or until steam is pouring out from under the lid.

7   Let the mussels cool. Remove the mussel meat from the shells and put it in a covered bowl or dish.

8   In a medium-sized bowl, whisk the eggs, milk, cream and mayonnaise. Set aside.

9   Melt the butter in a sauté pan over medium heat. Sauté the onions until they are translucent. Stir in the tarragon, salt and mussel meat. Set aside.

ASSEMBLY

10   Remove the crust from the oven. Put the cheese in the bottom and top with the mussels followed by the egg mixture. Bake for 60 to 75 minutes or until a knife inserted in the middle comes out clean.

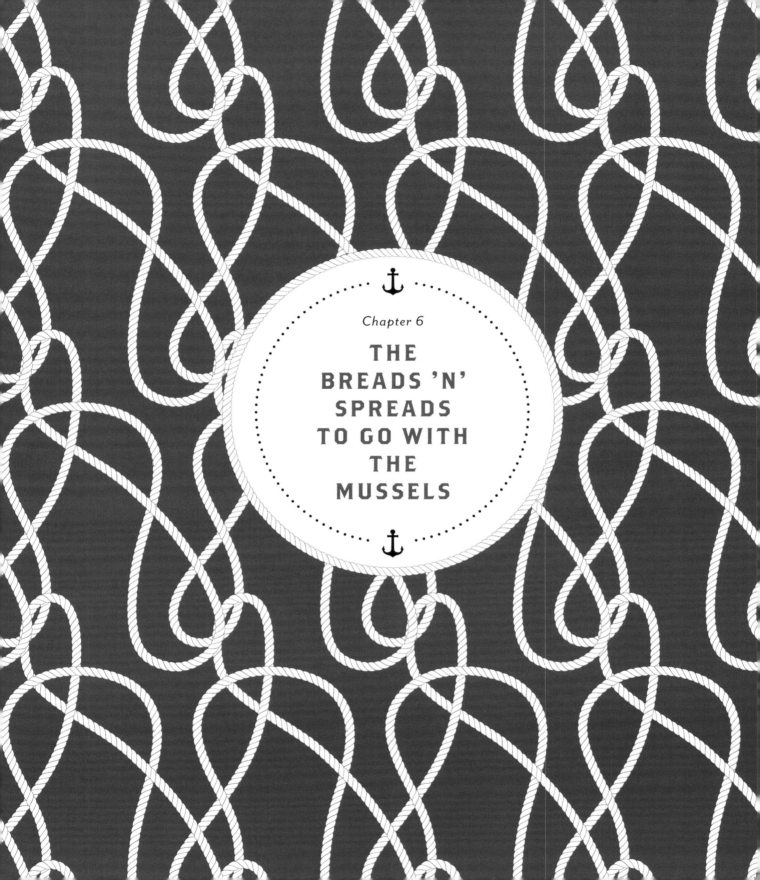

Chapter 6

THE BREADS 'N' SPREADS TO GO WITH THE MUSSELS

CHEESE AND THYME BISCUITS

{Makes 24 biscuits}

3 cups (750 mL) white all-
  purpose flour

6 tsp (30 mL) baking powder

1 tsp (5 mL) salt

1 Tbsp (15 mL) chopped fresh
  thyme

⅓ cup (80 mL) white sugar

⅓ cup (80 mL) vegetable oil

1 egg, lightly beaten

1½ cups (375 mL) buttermilk

2 Tbsp (30 mL) milk

½ cup (185 mL) grated extra old
  cheddar cheese

THIS VARIATION ON Linda's mom's famous biscuit recipe is greatly loved by her family. They ask her for her biscuits instead of presents. They are light, moist and fluffy but still have a beautiful consistency, and they absolutely taste the best right out of the oven with a slab of salted butter. The recipe is wonderful without the thyme and cheese if you prefer a plainer biscuit, or you can substitute old Gouda for the extra old cheddar.

1 Preheat your oven to 425°F (220°C).

2 Mix the flour, baking powder, salt and thyme in a medium-sized bowl with a fork.

3 In a separate bowl, combine the sugar, oil, egg, buttermilk and milk. Reserve 1 tsp (5 mL) of the milk for later.

4 Add the wet ingredients and the cheese to the bowl of dry ingredients. Knead the ingredients together about 15 to 25 times (not too much).

5 Roll out on a floured surface to about ¾ inch (2 cm) thick. Cut into circles about 1½ to 2 inches (4 to 5 cm) across and place on an insulated baking sheet. Linda's mom uses a small glass to cut the circles, but Linda has a pastry ring that does the trick. Brush the tops of the biscuits with the reserved milk.

6 Bake for 15 minutes until golden, and remove from the oven. Place on a cooling rack and serve with your favourite mussel soup.

SAVOURY POLENTA CAKES

{Makes 8 cakes}

8 cups (2 L) vegetable broth
   (packaged or homemade)
1 tsp (5 mL) salt
2 cups (500 mL) coarsely
   ground cornmeal
2 Tbsp (30 mL) butter
2 Tbsp (30 mL) chopped fresh
   thyme
1 Tbsp (15 mL) vegetable oil

POLENTA IS A dish that is common in the northern region of Italy. It is served as a starch similar to the way we use potatoes in North America. Polenta can be served soft or it can be left to firm up as we have done here.

■   ■

1   Pour the vegetable broth into a heavy-bottomed pot. Stir in the salt and bring to a boil. Once the broth reaches the boiling point, slowly add the cornmeal in a steady stream, whisking constantly to avoid lumps. Once the cornmeal is incorporated, turn the heat to low and stir continuously with a wooden spoon until the liquid is absorbed and the polenta begins to pull away from the side of the pot. This will take approximately 10 to 12 minutes.

2   Once the polenta has reached the desired consistency, remove from the heat and incorporate the butter and herbs.

3   Spread the polenta in an ungreased 9- × 13-inch (23 × 33 cm) pan and refrigerate uncovered until completely cooled.

4   When you are ready to serve, remove the polenta from the refrigerator and cut into 8 equal squares. Cut those squares into triangles or circles and set aside.

5   Add the oil to a non-stick frying pan and heat over medium-high heat until the oil begins to shimmer. Add the polenta triangles and cook on both sides until they just begin to turn golden brown and crispy. Serve hot.

PLOYE

{Makes 12 cakes}

1 cup (250 mL) buckwheat flour
1 cup (250 mL) white flour
3 tsp (15 mL) baking powder
1 tsp (5 mL) salt
1½ cups (375 mL) cold water
½ cup (125 mL) boiling water

PLOYE IS A traditional Acadian dish that originated in the Brayon region of northern New Brunswick and is still very popular today. It has only a few ingredients—all very affordable—which made this a good dish to add substance to meals in times when the food stores were low. Ploye was served with maple syrup, molasses or a pork spread called cretons. It usually accompanied all three meals.

1   Mix the buckwheat flour, white flour, baking powder and salt in a large bowl. Add the cold water and mix well. Let stand 5 minutes. Add the boiling water and mix vigorously. Let stand for another 5 minutes.

2   Use a 2 oz (60 mL) ladle to pour the batter into a hot dry skillet (cast iron works best). Quickly spread the batter in a circular motion so that it is quite thin. When the surface is dry and the ploye is covered with holes, it is ready to be removed from the pan.

3   Unlike pancakes, ploye is only cooked on one side. For best results, stir the batter between each ploye.

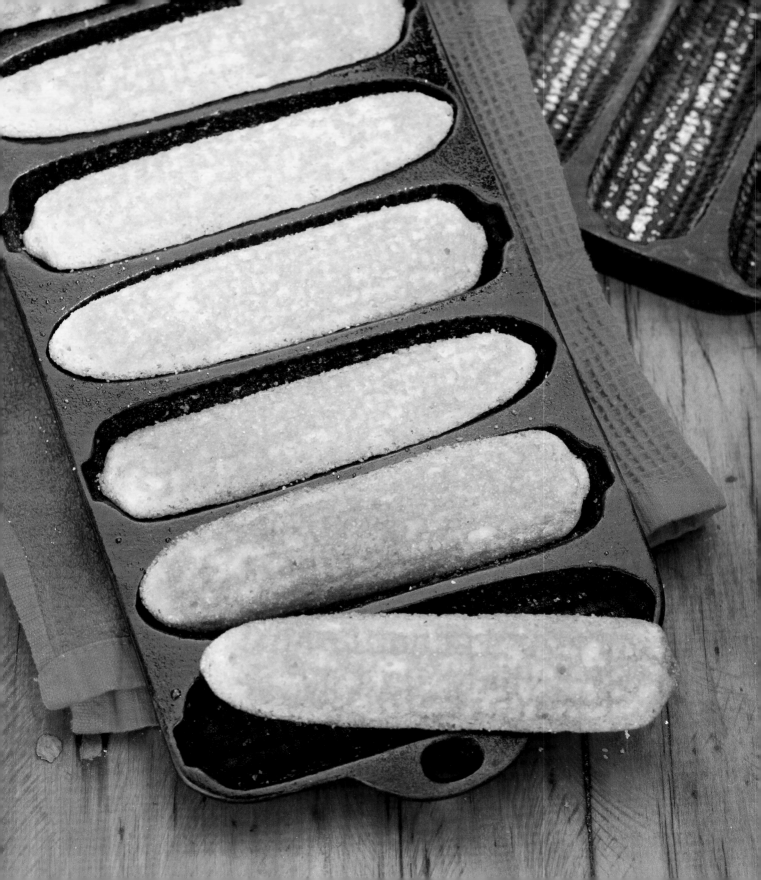

BUTTERMILK CORNBREAD MUFFINS

{Makes 12 muffins}

1 cup (250 mL) medium-ground cornmeal

1 cup (250 mL) flour

⅔ cup (160 mL) white sugar

3½ tsp (17.5 mL) baking powder

pinch of salt

1 cup (250 mL) buttermilk

1 egg, lightly beaten

⅓ cup (80 mL) canola oil

CORNBREAD IS ALWAYS a big hit at Alain's home. They serve it with soups and stews and use it as a topping for chili. Sometimes he makes it for breakfast and serves it hot with maple syrup, a variation on a traditional Maritime dish known as johnnycake. The addition of buttermilk gives it a slight tangy flavour.

1   Preheat the oven to 400°F (200°C).

2   Grease a muffin tin and set aside.

3   In a large bowl, combine the cornmeal, flour, white sugar, baking powder and salt. Mix well.

4   In a separate bowl, mix together the buttermilk, egg and canola oil. Make a well in the centre of the dry ingredients and pour in the wet mixture. Mix well.

5   Spoon the batter into the muffin tins. Place in the centre of the oven and bake for 25 to 30 minutes. The cornbread is ready when the tip of a knife inserted into the centre of the muffin comes out clean.

BANNOCK

{Makes 6 pieces}

3½ cups (875 mL) flour
2 Tbsp (30 mL) baking powder
1 tsp (5 mL) salt
1¼ cups (300 mL) cold water
¼ cup (60 mL) shortening

FUR TRADERS WERE the first to bring unleavened bread to Canada's First Nations. With little room in the canoes for transporting equipment and ingredients, bannock was the perfect solution. The fur traders simply mixed flour, water and animal fat and cooked it over an open fire. If an iron skillet wasn't available, the dough was wrapped around a stick and baked over the hot coals using a turning motion.

■   ■

1   In a large bowl, mix the flour, baking powder and salt. Slowly add the cold water and mix with your hands until the dough comes together and leaves the side of the bowl. Still using your hands, form the dough into a ball that is the same diameter as your frying pan.

2   Heat a large frying pan (cast iron works best) over medium-low heat. Add the shortening and allow it to melt, and then add the dough. Cover and cook until the bottom is golden brown (approximately 10 to 15 minutes).

3   Flip the bannock onto a plate. Add more shortening to the pan if needed. Return the bannock to the pan, cover and cook until the other side is golden.

4   Remove from heat and cut into six wedges.

BUTTERY ASIAGO BREAD STICKS

{Makes 36 fingers}

1 loaf of good-quality unsliced
 white bread
½ lb (250 g) butter, melted
½ cup (125 mL) finely grated
 Asiago cheese

ONCE YOU TRY this rich, buttery, cheesy crouton, Alain guarantees you will never add a hard, dry, store-bought crouton to your soup or salad again! They really only take a few moments to prepare, and they will take your dish to a whole new level.

1 Preheat the oven to 350°F (175°C).

2 Slice the ends, top, bottom and sides off the loaf so that you are left with no crust. Slice the bread into 9 equal slices, and cut each slice into 4 fingers. You should have a total of 36 fingers.

3 Dip three sides of each finger in the melted butter and then into the Asiago cheese.

4 Place the sticks with the undipped side down on a baking sheet lined with parchment paper. Bake for approximately 20 minutes or until golden brown.

5 Store leftover bread sticks in an airtight container.

GOAT CHEESE CROSTINI

{Makes 20}

SPREAD

¾ cup (185 mL) goat cheese

⅓ cup (80 mL) cream cheese

8 stems chives, chopped

2 sprigs oregano, stems removed,
 chopped

½ tsp (2.5 mL) cracked black
 pepper

CROSTINI

1 French baguette

4 Tbsp (60 mL) olive oil

salt

THESE CROSTINI ARE a great accompaniment to homemade soups and salads. They also make nice hors d'oeuvres topped with a toasted pecan and a drizzle of honey or a fresh fig and balsamic reduction.

■　　　　　　　■

SPREAD

1 Use a hand mixer to incorporate the goat cheese and the cream cheese until smooth. Add the chives, oregano and pepper, and combine until smooth.

2 Refrigerate for 30 minutes.

CROSTINI

3 Preheat your oven to 400°F (200°C).

4 Slice your baguette on the bias into slices that are about a ½-inch (1 cm) thick. Place on a baking sheet lined with parchment paper, brush with olive oil, and then turn over and brush the other side. Sprinkle with salt.

5 Bake for 4 minutes on each side or until golden brown.

6 Remove from the oven and cool.

ASSEMBLY

7 Spread the cheese mixture on the crostini and place under the broiler to melt the cheese.

MAÎTRE D'HÔTEL BUTTER

{Makes 2 cups (500 mL)}

½ cup (125 mL) chopped parsley

2 cups (500 mL) salted butter, softened

¼ cup (60 mL) lemon juice

4 drops Worcestershire sauce

pinch of pepper

THIS BUTTER IS a classic that has been used for many years. In fact, it is one of the first things cooks are taught how to make in culinary school. It is a great accompaniment to seafood, chicken and beef. I like to keep a few rolls of it in my freezer at all times. It adds that little something special to finish a dish.

1   Add the parsley to the softened butter and mix well, using a spatula. Add the lemon juice, Worcestershire sauce and pepper and mix thoroughly.

2   Divide the butter in half; roll each half in waxed paper and refrigerate. Once the butter is hard, you can slice it as needed.

3   To store the butter for a longer time, you can freeze it but it should be placed in a sealed bag.

ROSEMARY DIJON BUTTER

{Makes 2 cups (500 mL)}

4 sprigs rosemary, stems removed

1 lb (500 g) salted butter, softened

2 Tbsp (30 mL) Dijon mustard

¼ cup (60 mL) lemon juice

½ tsp (2.5 mL) ground pepper

THIS BUTTER IS one of our favourite butters for serving with mussels. Alain just melts it and serves it alongside dishes for dipping. It is also very good placed underneath the skin of a chicken before roasting to keep the meat flavourful and moist.

1   Place the rosemary in a food processor and pulse to release the natural oils. Add the butter and process until almost smooth. Add the Dijon, lemon juice and pepper, and continue to process until the mixture has a smooth consistency.

2   Roll the butter in waxed paper and store in the freezer until needed.

MOLASSES BUTTER

{Makes 1½ cups (375 mL)}

1 cup (250 mL) softened salted
  butter
½ cup (125 mL) molasses

Molasses was once a staple in all Maritime homes. It was affordable and had many uses. In Alain's house, it was a real treat to get a jar of peanut butter, which was expensive for them. To make the peanut butter last longer, his dad mixed it half and half with molasses! Alain's version of molasses butter is very simple but comforting. Try it on biscuits or cornbread hot from the oven.

1   Place the butter and molasses in a stand mixer and whip until nice and smooth.

HONEY BASIL BUTTER

{Makes 1½ cups (375 mL)}

1 lb (500 g) salted butter
20 fresh basil leaves
½ cup (125 mL) honey

THIS BUTTER IS a great accompaniment to seafood, fish and chicken. Wherever possible, try to buy your honey from a local source. Alain is proud to keep his own hives; in the end, beekeeping benefits us all.

1   Place the butter and basil in a food processor and process until almost smooth. Gradually add the honey. Continue to process slowly until it reaches the desired consistency. Taste to make sure that it is to your liking. Add more honey if you feel it needs to be sweeter for the dish you are making or more basil if you are leaning toward savoury.

MAPLE CRANBERRY BUTTER

{Makes 2 cups (500 mL)}

⅔ cup (160 mL) dried cranberries
1 lb (500 g) salted butter
¼ cup (60 mL) maple syrup
1 tsp (5 mL) milled black pepper

MAPLE AND CRANBERRIES are two popular products in the Atlantic Provinces. On a recent trip to Germany, Alain was asked to incorporate them both into one dish. He didn't want to do something conventional, so he developed a butter to be served with bannock. This butter is a great accompaniment for mussels or fish, or it can be used to baste pork.

1 Place the dried cranberries in a food processor and pulse until they are finely ground. Add the butter, maple syrup and pepper, and whip until nice and smooth.

2 Chill before serving (this is best made a day ahead).

ACKNOWLEDGEMENTS

I want to say a special thank you to Guy Delorme and Chef Jean Paul Grellier. These two gentlemen were my instructors in culinary school and it was them who gave me the tools that I needed to succeed, they are the same gentlemen who continue to inspire me to this day.

　　—Alain

This book is also for the two people who were instrumental in guiding me to become a cook, Ada Greene and Ruth Dunch. Ada is my late grandmother who gave me my first mixing spoon and taught me the basics without me even realizing it. Ruth, an accomplished home economist, was my second mother. During the years I lived with her family in Bermuda, she introduced me to ingredients and cooking methods that enriched my knowledge and helped me on my journey to become a competent cook.

　　—Linda

To Chef Michael Smith for agreeing to write the foreword of our mussel cookbook. Secondly, we want to acknowledge his continuous promotion and support of P.E.I. mussels and the mussel industry. He has helped foster our project at its inception and we are so appreciative of his support.

To Perry Jackson, our photographer for this book, for the beautiful and creative photography together with his great eye in assisting with the set ups for the shoots. We also discovered that he was an excellent taste tester for our recipes in between the shots.

To the Mussel Industry Council who have shared with us some of their wonderful images and also their encouragement to write this book.

To Len Currie at Confederation Cove Mussels in Borden P.E.I. for his generosity in supplying our beautiful P.E.I. mussels for the photo shoot even in squeaky boxes from PEI to NS. They showcased extremely well in the photographs.

To our Chef friends who agreed to contribute their national versions of mussels Frank Widmar from Switzerland, Jose Duarte in Boston via Peru, and Mario D'Antonio in Italy.

Thanks for the very appetizing looking Ploye photo by Mylène Violette.

To the hard working mussel farmers on P.E.I. whose labours produce amazing mussels every season of the year. You are tenacious, innovative and produce the most wonderful tasting mussels that we all could ever ask for.

INDEX